MANNA from DEVON
COOKING SCHOOL

WOOD FIRED FLATBREADS & PANCAKES

by David & Holly Jones

This edition is published by Manna from Devon
Fir Mount House · Higher Contour Road · Kingswear · TQ6 0DE

mannafromdevon.com · info@mannafromdevon.com

Publishers - David and Holly Jones
Design - Simon E Blogg · Cherub Consultancy Ltd
Commissioned Photography - Nick Hook · Nick Hook Photography
Commissioned Art Work - Sue Bown

A CIP record for this book is available from the British Library.

ISBN 978-1-5272-0217-7

Colour Reproduction by Gutenberg Press Ltd
Printed in Malta

Publisher's Note:
Every care has been taken to ensure that all recipes and instructions in this book are accurate and safe.
However Manna from Devon and any other persons who have been involved in production of this publication
cannot accept responsibility or liability for any omissions or errors, inadvertent or otherwise,
that may be found in the recipes or text nor for any problems, injury, damage or loss to persons or property
that may arise as a result of preparing one of these recipes or from advice in this book.

Notes:
Recipe quantities are written in metric, imperial and standard cup sizes where appropriate.
Do not mix measurements when following a recipe.
Spoon measurements are level unless otherwise stated.
tsp = teaspoon · tbsp = tablespoon

Refractory Dome

Insulation

Fire / Oven Chamber

Refractory Floor Insulation

Flue

Doorway

S. Bou

MANNA from DEVON
COOKING SCHOOL

INTRODUCTION 7

ABOUT THE AUTHORS 11

ABOUT YOUR OVEN *and making fire* 15

OVEN HEAT 19

ESSENTIAL EQUIPMENT 25

INGREDIENTS 29

MAKING DOUGH 35

RECIPES 41

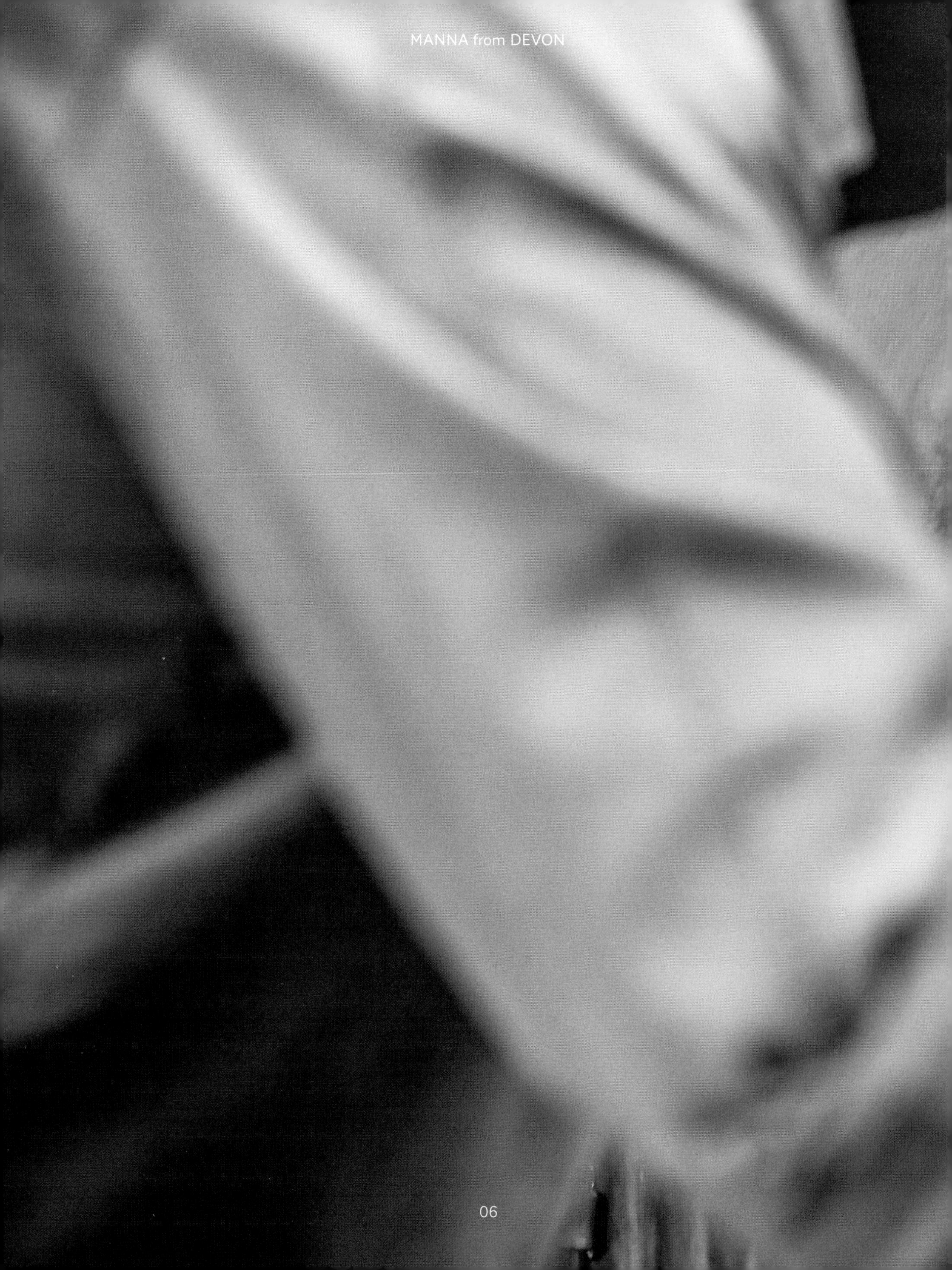

INTRODUCTION

INTRODUCTION

Pretty much the first thing anyone cooks when they get a wood fired oven is pizza. And why not? Pizza is great and the best pizza is one baked in a wood fired oven. Unfortunately, for some, that's as far as they get. Noooo! Your wood fired oven is the most versatile piece of kit in your outdoor cooking armoury and pizza is merely the tip of a very, very big iceberg. Remember, for thousands of years no ovens existed except wood fired ones so every traditional baked or roasted dish started in a wood fired oven.

In this book we set out to explore some of those recipes which are a bit like pizza but not actually pizza. Almost every culture has created some form of flatbreads or pancakes. Oatcakes from Scotland, Chapatti from India, Tortilla from Mexico or Injera from Ethiopia all qualify. Apart from being flat they all have one consistent characteristic; they cook in minutes. They will all have developed when simplicity of cooking was vital and ovens were simple or non-existent. These breads were cooked over a flame or in simple earth ovens.

We've taken inspiration from our travels and the classes we run at Manna from Devon to put together 24 recipes which you'll want to use over and over again. We absolutely love how quick and simple it is to create these breads and pancakes and how much people enjoy having them fresh from the oven – heavenly.

Flatbreads and pancakes make great brunches, lunches, snacks, picnics, starters, even desserts and also do a great job in taking out some of the energy of the oven so you can then cook something that requires a lesser heat. It's very satisfying to have such a range of dishes at your fingertips made with the most basic of ingredients - flour, water, yeast and salt.

We've written our recipes based on what works in our oven, what our friends and students at the cooking school like and what we know you can recreate at home. We've tested and retested them in our ovens which have a good thermal mass so retain the heat well. Obviously each oven will have different properties so you'll need to practise on yours to find out what works best.

We've also written down our way of telling the temperature in your oven – or feeling the temperature really. Before you start cooking, do make sure you read this bit as all the recipes refer back to it.

If you don't have a wood fired oven, don't worry - you can still cook them in your conventional oven; just follow the temperature guidelines. We use a piece of polished granite on the oven shelves to provide some extra oomph from below. For those recipes requiring high heat turn your oven up to maximum. Things will take a little longer but will still turn out fine.

"If you have not yet attended one of the wood fired oven cooking courses at Manna from Devon, you are missing out; you may end up thinking that a wood fired oven is just for pizza. That would be a huge mistake!

Holly and David are without a doubt the masters of wood fired cooking in the UK. Their first book is a must for any one starting out. I have no doubt that future books will be just as fantastic."

Jay Emery, Master Oven Builder & MD of Bushman Wood Fired Ovens

ABOUT THE AUTHORS

ABOUT THE AUTHORS

We are David and Holly Jones and we run Manna from Devon Cooking School on the beautiful South Devon coast in England. We LOVE, LOVE, LOVE cooking in our wood fired ovens (at the last count, we had 6 of them!) and teaching people how to use their own – currently we're the only cooking school in the UK to teach people how to use their ovens to the extent that we do.

We don't have a traditional catering background although David is very proud of his cookery 'O' level and Holly trained at Leith's School of Food and Wine in London for a year. We have degrees in philosophy and modern languages and short service commissions in the British Army and the Royal Navy between us so it's certainly not the normal route into cooking!

Our aim is to send our cooking school students away with the confidence, knowledge and belief that they can cook lovely food at home. Like most things, confidence in cooking comes from doing it and using the right tool for the right job so we'll show you what to use and how to use it and let you practise. We want to provide a welcoming environment for all our classes and let everyone get stuck in so that they can learn from us and each other without worrying about the mess.

Wood fired oven cooking is big news in the cooking world – people tell us they love it because of the great flavours in the food, the fact that it's a really sociable way to cook and the connection it gives to generations of cooks who've gone before in this very traditional and intuitive way of providing food. It is much more than turning on a knob and waiting for your oven to heat up. You need all of your senses working to make the most of it – touch, hearing, sight, smell and taste. You really need to feel what's going on.

We have been teaching people how to use their wood fired ovens since 2010 both here at the cooking school and all over the UK and Europe. We've travelled through Europe, Asia and the US checking out how people cook on fire, talking to them and learning their technique.

Our first wood fired book – the Wood Fired Oven Cook Book – was released in 2012 by Aquamarine, an imprint of Anness Publishing, and is still going strong. So exciting!

We'd love to hear from you so do contact us with questions at info@mannafromdevon.com . We're also all over social media – Facebook, Twitter, Instagram, Pinterest and Tumblr. We love seeing pictures of your ovens & your cooking and hearing of where you are in the world – you never know, when we're next passing, we could well drop in!

And of course you can also come and join us on one of our cooking courses here in lovely South Devon.

Happy cooking everyone!
David and Holly

"...without wishing to gush,
if you are getting a wood burning oven you really
should do the Manna from Devon course.
In fact, I'd say it's essential"

Xanthe Clay, food writer of the Daily Telegraph

Did you know:
The word refractory
comes from the Latin, 'refractarius',
meaning obstinate or resistant to change.

ABOUT YOUR OVEN
and making fire

A LITTLE ABOUT OVENS
AND MAKING FIRE

Did you know:
The word refractory comes from the Latin, 'refractarius', meaning obstinate or resistant to change.

Almost all wood fired ovens have a refractory element to them; i.e. the part of the oven which absorbs heat without burning, melting or bending. In some cases this is just the floor of the oven and in traditional ovens it's the whole material from which the oven is made, be it clay, brick or concrete. Metals are not refractory since they melt or distort at relatively low temperatures.

An oven with a large amount of refractory will be capable of much greater heat stability than one with a small amount. This increases the versatility of the oven, making it capable of cooking dishes from meringues to pizza, to batches of loaves and pots of traditional stews braised for 18 hours.

However, the greater the amount of refractory the longer the oven will take to reach a state of stability and the heavier it will be. Luckily we are now able to get wood fired ovens which fit every need from super portable to heavy-duty work horses.

Whichever type of oven you have, it's always important to preheat the refractory material before you start to cook. The refractory (sometimes referred to as thermal mass) acts as a heat sink, retaining heat energy and providing a stable cooking environment. This is the case even if you are just heating pizza stones in the floor of the oven.

Here's how to make a fire in and heat a traditional refractory oven.

- Create a hearth of fairly large split logs (about 10cm/4" diameter) to hold the fire in place while it gets established. Build this near the front of your oven, 8-10cm/3–4" behind the flue. Initially your fire needs plenty of oxygen, building it too far into the oven will stifle the flames.
- Create a 'jenga' stack of small split logs (up to 2.5cm/1" diameter) leaving plenty of space for oxygen and flames to move between the wood.
- Add larger logs to the top of your stack, still leaving room for air movement.
- Place 1 firelighter at the base of the 'jenga' stack.
- Light the firelighter and leave the whole thing until the wood is burning well.
- Push the whole fire back into the centre of the oven. The fire should now be hitting the centre of the dome putting energy into the oven roof and heating the floor at the same time.
- Add more wood as necessary to keep the fire burning brightly. Don't be afraid to make an enormous fire during this oven heating cycle. Students at the cooking school have told us that they haven't made a fire as big as ours before so be brave and go for some big heat.
- Watch the top of your dome inside the oven. Initially it will become black as the fire coats it with soot. As the dome of the oven begins to saturate with heat the soot burns off and the dome returns to its original colour. This is known as clearing. You'll see the oven clear from the top down and bottom up as heat spreads evenly throughout the dome. It's a good idea to wait until the dome is completely clear before cooking.
- Once the dome is clear push the fire to the back or off to one side of the oven to clear the floor for cooking.
- Keep the fire burning for a very hot oven; 0 – 2 Mississippi, or allow it to die down for hot or moderate temperatures.
- In a full refractory oven with good insulation you can expect the oven to retain heat for 12 hours or more.
- For refractory concrete ovens built for domestic purposes we'd expect them to be heated up, clear and stable in an hour or so. A brick built oven will take longer because the depth of refractory brick is greater. In a handmade, clay oven expect to need to heat the oven for longer.
- If we are cooking with a fire burning then the door is usually off the oven. This allows maximum oxygen in to keep the fire burning and maximum exhaust fumes out. When cooking with the fire out, we'll keep the door off if we want the oven a little cooler or place the door on but ajar if we want the temperature to build whilst still allowing fumes to escape.

OVEN HEAT

HOW HOT IS THE OVEN?

This is the question we are asked more than any other here at the cooking school on our wood fired classes. The answer is always – "it depends".

There are a variety of ways of taking the temperature in your wood fired oven and different ovens will have different heat retention capabilities. You really need to work with yours to see how it reacts.

In one of our ovens we have internal thermometers which will tell us the temperatures beneath the floor and on top of the insulating layers. We also have an electronic zapper which will give the temperature at a given spot where the laser is pointing.

To be honest we've got 2 of these gadgets; one cost £60 when we started all those years ago and is still going strong. We have another that cost £15 last year and the difference in temperatures given is about 15-20 degrees so it's best to spend some money on your zapper in the "you get what you pay for" school of thought.

If you think about it, your thermometer can only tell you the temperature of where it is or where it's pointing. Here at the cooking school, we really try to encourage people to think differently about temperatures and to cook more intuitively, to develop a feeling for the oven and its heat – yes it's hot but how hot? And what can you do with that heat?

So how do we test the heat? What we do is see how many seconds we need to hold our hand in the oven before our fingers start to tingle? This gives a rough idea of the air temperature which is really what we're interested in because that's the temperature your recipe is talking about. The tingling is basically a sign that your fingers are starting to cook. When you feel your fingers start to tingle, take your hand out of the oven - we are NOT (!!) encouraging you to stick your hands in the oven and leave them in there for as long as possible; it's not a test of your pain threshold.

Unless you've got a thermometer dangling in the middle of your oven, you will find it difficult to measure the air temperature by any other means than the hand test which is why we'd like you to start developing a "feel" for your oven and really start thinking about what it is you're feeling.

If you can't hold your fingers in there at all or only for a second, then the oven is properly good and hot and still has a fire burning inside, it means you can cook thin flatbreads in no time at all - something like a pitta. If you can leave them in for 5 seconds or so, then you can cook things that need longer time in the oven or a gentler heat to bake through - things like our sweet flat breads or the rye crackers which are really just drying out.

In addition to the air temperature, you also need to have built up some heat in the thermal mass of your oven so that the oven is stable - not heating up and cooling down very quickly if there's no fire inside. We get our ovens to a stable temperature by keeping a fire burning inthe oven for a good hour or so. This means the thermal mass has absorbed a lot of heat and we can still cook in the oven without a fire. This is great news as the flat breads will cook evenly without getting a smokey flavour – just what we're looking for.

The best way to test how much thermal mass your oven has and how long it will hold the heat is experience – burn a good fire for an hour or so, take the temperatures and see how long it takes for them to drop. As we said it will be different for every oven.

Here's how you carry out the hand test –

1 Put your hand in the oven about 5cm/2inches above the oven floor where you'll be cooking but not touching the oven itself.

2 Start counting as if you're in a parachute jump – "One Mississippi, two Mississippi, three Mississippi, four Mississippi, five Mississippi, six Mississippi...."

So what are your tingling fingers actually telling you? Well let us explain:

0 Mississippi – if you can't get your hand in the oven at all, then the air temp is super hot and will be more than 400°C/750°F. At this temperature, you can cook pizzas, pitta breads, some other thinner flatbreads, prawns, squid, fish fillets etc. You need to keep an eye on whatever it is you're cooking as it can go from perfect to err, well, black as soon as you've turned your back. You'll only ever achieve this temperature with a good fire burning in the oven.

One Mississippi – Between 300°C/570°F and 400°C/750°F. If you can keep your hand in for the count of One Mississippi but no more, you're good to cook pittas, prawns, scallops, minute steaks, lamb kebabs or koftas. Again, keep an eye on things as it all happens pretty quickly. A fire or bed of hot embers will be needed for this.

Two Mississippi – Between 275°C/520°F and 300°C/570°F. Still pretty high here but we can get bigger things in the oven without risking them blackening before cooking through so think about cooking thin flatbreads, fish and dishes which can start hot as long as the oven falls in temperature fairly quickly. These might include spatchcocked chicken, butterflied leg of lamb, barbeque chicken wings and thighs, chipolata sausages, trays of veggies for roasting etc. We have a piece of good wide aluminium foil on hand in case things are colouring up too quickly.

Three Mississippi – Between 250°C/480°F and 275°C/520°F. At three Mississippi, things are calmer and you can do thicker flatbreads such as foccacia, pissaladiere and khachapuri, some larger steaks (we do a 1.5kg piece of rump steak 3cm thick – perfect at this heat).

Four Mississippi – Between 220°C/430°F and 250°C/480°F. This is your bread setting so use it for baking bigger loaves such as sourdoughs, wholemeals, and flatbreads requiring a gentler heat. Also great for bigger chunks of roast meats like legs of lamb, whole chickens, ribs of beef.

Five Mississippi – Between 175°C/350°F and 220°C/430°F. Cooling down now so the oven is great for cakes, pastries, sweet doughs, crackers.

Six Mississippi – less than 175°C/350°F. Cooling nicely but still with a lot of retained heat if your oven has a good thermal mass so perfect for packing in those slow braises such as shoulders of lamb or pork, stocks, fruit cakes, rice puddings; just shut the door and come back later.

As for the fire itself, we probably only have a fire burning at 0-2 Mississippi – this will give a good grilling effect and some smokiness. At 3 Mississippi, we'll be cooking with a good bed of embers in the oven but no flames as such and are more reliant on the retained heat in the thermal mass. From 4 Mississippi onwards, it's just about retained heat and you can shut the door for longer, even cooking.

We know this is a lot to take in especially after we've all been cooking on electric and gas ovens for so long. If you practise the "feel" for what's going on in the oven every time you light it up, you will soon develop an understanding and know instinctively when to put things in. Remember people have been cooking with fire for thousands of years and it's only in the past 150 years or so that we've become reliant on electric or gas ovens with temperature control. Try to get out of the habit of thinking of the temperature and start thinking about how much energy is in the oven and it all becomes a much more intuitive process.

"One Mississippi,
two Mississippi, three Mississippi,
four Mississippi, five Mississippi,
six Mississippi...."

ESSENTIAL EQUIPMENT

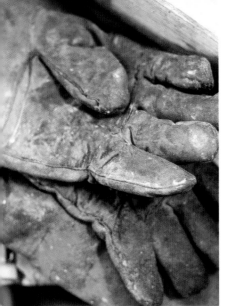

ESSENTIAL EQUIPMENT

If you are going to cook successfully with your wood fired oven, there are some bits of kit you really need. All of it can be bought online. Here are our can't-do-withouts –

Your hands will be in and out of a very hot oven so they need protection. We use welders' gauntlets which are long enough to go up your forearms and flexible enough to hold things easily.

A gadget to test how dry your wood is - a moisture meter in fact. Very easy to use, you just take the lid off and shove the 2 prongs into the bit of wood in question. The moisture count in your wood wants to be definitely less than 20% and ideally less than 15%.

We use eco-lighters to light the fire; ours are made of champagne case packing shavings and candlewax so no nasty chemicals.

Make sure you have a good box of matches, kept in a sealable box so they don't get damp – we use a plastic one with a snappable lid.

A laser thermometer for testing temperatures all round your oven.

A probe thermometer for testing the internal temperatures of meat and loaves of bread just out of the oven.

Dough scrapers – crucial in your bread-making. They are basically a bit of flat plastic with a straight side and a side with rounded corners to get the dough out of bowls and for cutting through the dough. We also use them for cleaning dough, both dry and wet off our work table and for scraping dough off our fingers if the phone's going. They are so much more useful than a knife when you are making bread.

Peels and brushes
A peel is a flat paddle made from either wood or metal use for putting bread on to the oven floor.

• We bought a lovely wooden peel which unfortunately split on its first use but it's still very handy for placing loaves in the oven.

• We keep one peel as a dirty peel for placing pieces of wood on the fire and for moving embers around. It's covered in ash and soot and if it is ever needed for anything else, gets a good wash in hot soapy water first.

• A large metal peel for flat breads and pizzas. Load the flat breads on to the well floured peel and then shuffle it off on to the oven floor; remember to use a little flour or semolina underneath the dough or your flatbread won't be going anywhere. Don't put too much flour or semolina on to your peel otherwise it will burn on the oven floor and blacken your flatbread base. We have a very nifty metal peel with lots of holes in it which means most of the flour drops through before getting on to the oven floor.

• A smaller metal peel for moving things around in the oven.

A bristle brush for brushing the oven floor clear of flour.

• A large metal brush for cleaning the floor as and when necessary and especially if anything has burnt on to the floor. We also cover this with a damp cloth and use it as a mop to clean the oven floor before baking on it once we've moved the fire to the side or back of the oven.

A blowpipe used to blow oxygen into the base of the fire if we need to get it going and also very useful for blowing away any ash that's on the oven floor so it's clean for cooking. It's not very high-tec – it's just a metal pole from the inside of an old wardrobe with one end bashed almost shut with a hammer and in the other end we put a Hozelock tap connector so we can blow down the pipe without burning our lips.

A couple of axes for splitting logs into smaller pieces and kindling and a sturdy chopping block for splitting the logs on - just a big bit of tree trunk with a flat surface.

Plenty of very dry seasoned hardwood logs cut into 25cm/10" lengths and stored undercover on their sides. We get ours from our friend Edward the farmer at the top of the hill. He stores our wood for 3 years so it is really dry – less than 15% on our moisture meter. It is a combination of hard woods – round here we get oak, beech, sycamore. Don't use soft wood such as pine or eucalyptus as they spit and burn away very quickly. If you can't source good quality dry wood locally to you, there are now a variety of suppliers online who will deliver a pallet to your kerbside.

Buckets – we use a plastic bucket full of water every time we cook as a fire bucket just in case of emergencies. We also have a large metal bucket to put hot ash into when we're emptying the oven if we just want to cook with retained heat.

Fire extinguisher and fire blanket – just in case.

First aid kit – always useful when using axes and fire.

Rolling pin – we have a selection of wooden rolling pins for rolling out the flatbreads. Get the widest one you can find.

Kitchen papers – make sure you get some wide, heavy duty aluminium foil to cover things up if they are browning too quickly in the oven. Also some good quality wide baking parchment.

And finally a selection of good sturdy pans.

• We use cast iron or steel pans for use at high temperatures and enamel pans and ceramic dishes at lower gentler temperatures. Pots and pans like these are quite easy to pick up at car boot sales, yard sales or charity or junk shops as the type of pan we want – heavy and sturdy – are not what most people now have in their conventional kitchens.

• Remember not to use anything that is too thin as it will buckle nor anything non-stick as the lining will be damaged.

INGREDIENTS

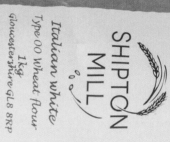

SHIPTON
MILL

Italian white
Type 00 wheat flour
1kg
Gloucestershire GL8 8RP

INGREDIENTS

As far as flat breads go, you just start with the most basic of ingredients –

FLOUR · SALT · YEAST · WATER

Flour

Our flour comes from Shipton Mill in Gloucestershire, the flour of choice for most artisan bread makers. They have a great online ordering service at Flour Direct so it's easy to get hold of their flour wherever you are in the UK. If you're further afield, seek out your best available flour. We use -

• Strong White: multipurpose bread flour with strong gluten.
• 00 Flour: milled from hard wheat, very fine with a softer gluten and typically producing lighter, bubblier breads. Ideal for pizza
  and many other flatbreads.
• Stoneground wholewheat flour: adds texture, flavour, colour and nutrition to any bread but leads to denser doughs so use
  sparingly where lightness of texture is important.
• Plain flour: softer and with less gluten; perfect in pancakes but also used in unleavened breads.
• Rye Flour: low in gluten but great flavour, really nutritious and essential in many Scandinavian and Eastern European breads
• Chickpea or Gram flour: gluten free but suitable for batters.

Salt

Salt is essential in most breads and we use a fine seasalt when making yeasted doughs as it distributes evenly throughout the doughs. Also it doesn't cut through the crucial gluten that you've worked so hard to develop. If you want an extra crunchy saltiness on top of your flatbreads – like on a foccaccia – we would use the fabulous Cornish sea salt – lovely crystals either in plain, err, salty flavour or with lots of other combinations such as chilli, garlic, lemon & thyme and smoked salt.

Yeast

Bakers love to argue about the relative merits of fast acting yeast, dried active yeast and fresh yeast. I find the fast acting stuff gives as good a result as anything else and beats the rest hands down for convenience.

Here at the cooking school, we use Doves Farm Quick Yeast – it's reliable, easy to get hold of, mixes into the flour well without needing advance hydration, has a good shelf life and stores easily in a sealed plastic box in the fridge.

The recipes have been written to use this instant, fast acting yeast but if you prefer to use fresh, just double the weight of the instant.

Water

Well we have to admit to being in luck in South Devon – we have beautiful, fresh soft water with no obvious flavour of chlorine and it comes straight out of the tap. If yours isn't so delicious or is very hard, you might consider a water softener or bottled spring water.

Remember 1 millilitre of water (or milk) weighs 1 gram so we find it easier to weigh the water needed for each recipe rather than measure it in a measuring jug. If you want to try this method, it's easy to do; just convert ml into g.

"A very welcoming place and team
I learned sooo much in one day... I want a wood fired oven now !!!
Recommended 100%"

Sara Felix, Ashburton Cookery School Student

"Holly & David are an inspiration
in the wood fired oven cooking field
and amazing hosts!

Their passion really shows in their workshops
which are perfectly paced through demonstrations
and doing and balanced with just the right
amount of information and informality.

It really is a feast for the senses
and I can thoroughly recommend a day with them
to see the huge potential and endless possibilities
from cooking in a wood fired oven."

Sam Ward, Catering Manager - Collaton St Mary Primary School

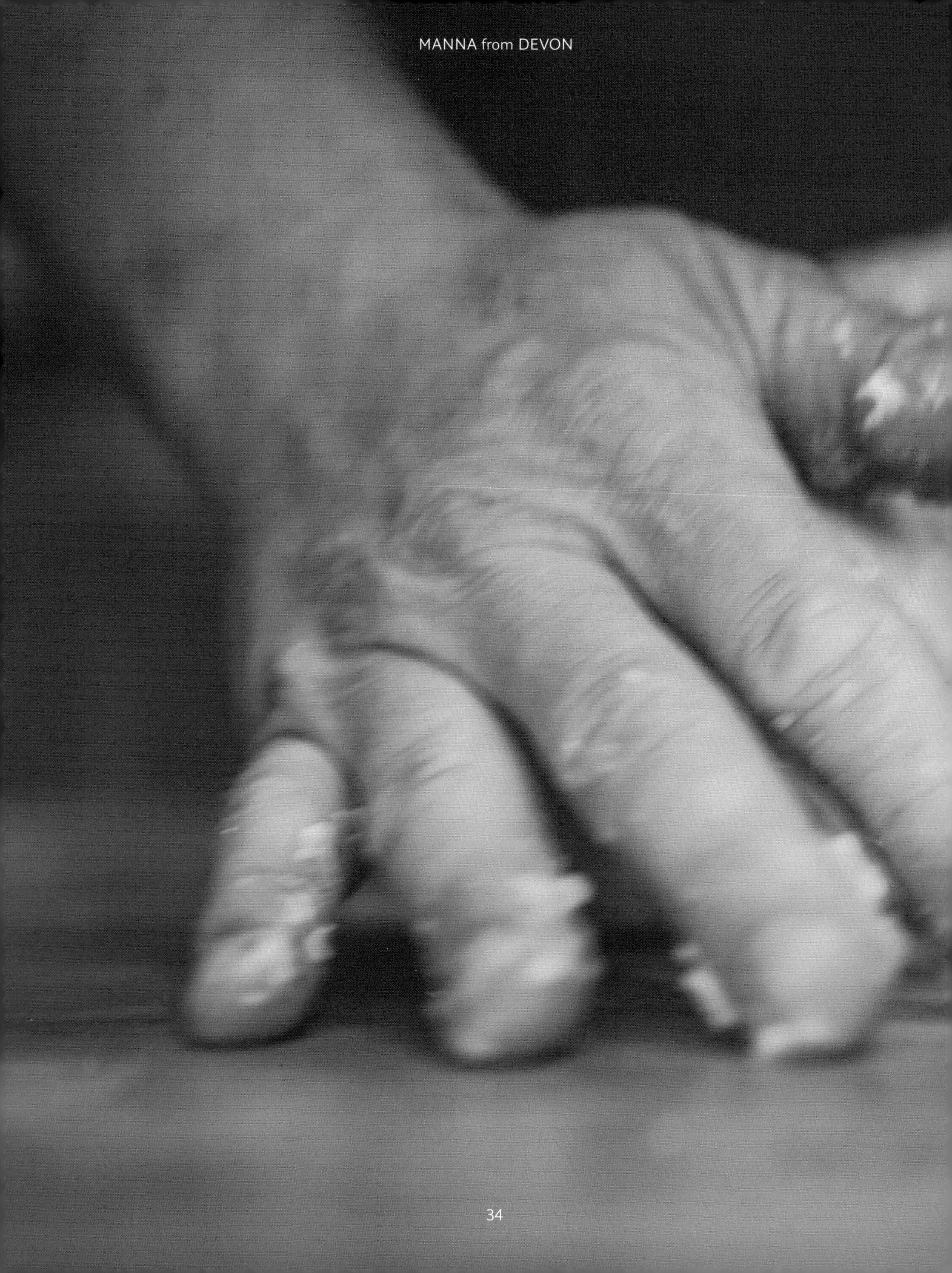

MAKING DOUGH

LET'S GO MAKE SOME DOUGH!
ADD SOME WATTER, NOW IT'S BATTER!

So goes a traditional nursery rhyme which I just made up. But it sort of sums up the simplicity of making flatbreads and pancakes; always some sort of flour and liquid, sometimes runny, sometimes not, sometimes yeasted, sometimes not.

Bread Dough ... The Basic Steps

Here's how to make bread:

• **Mix flour, water, salt. Add yeast or raising agent for lightness.** *(Yes, that's all you need)*

• **Stretch it a bit to make it stronger.** *(Kneading bread is a mini workout and quite relaxing)*

• **Leave it to ferment to develop flavour and texture.** *(Take a break after all that hard work)*

• **Shape it.** *(Into any of a million shapes, a chance to be creative)*

• **Leave it to become light and airy.** *(Take a break after all that hard work)*

• **Bake it** *(The oven does this bit. You just put it in, leave it and take it out again)*

So none of that sounds too taxing. Some of the doughs in this book are unleavened (i.e. no yeast or raising agent), some don't need any kneading, some don't get a second rising (even simpler), but the basic steps kind of stay the same.

So why don't we all bake our own bread? …. mostly due to the misconceptions routinely attached to baking:

• *It requires heaps of very specific knowledge and skills. (See above)*
• *Handling dough is really tricky. (It is true that handling some dough well requires a bit of practice, but doing anything well requires a bit of practice)*
• *It requires the temperature to be just right. (Bread is popular in both Africa and Alaska and bakers there manage to bake some fantastic bread)*
• *Yeast is very temperamental. (Maybe it was once when it was harvested from the top of beer vats but modern yeast isn't)*
• *It takes ages. (Definitely not for many of the quick breads in this book)*
• *My hands are too cold (Unless you have a circulatory condition or are suffering from hypothermia, your hands are the same temperature as everyone else's give or take a few points of 1 degree)*
• *It won't be as good as the bread I buy. (If you buy industrial supermarket bread this is not true. If you buy bread from an experienced artisan bakery this will be true for the first few months of making your own, then your bread will be as good as theirs and you'll have the satisfaction of having made it yourself and it will be cheaper)*

So come on, enough with the excuses. Get a bag of flour and get baking!

"Amazing 2 day course! Feeling incredibly inspired to try out so many new things.
Who would have thought you could cook so many different things in a wood fired oven?
Thank you David & Holly for sharing your passion for food xx"

Emma Darby, Manna from Devon student

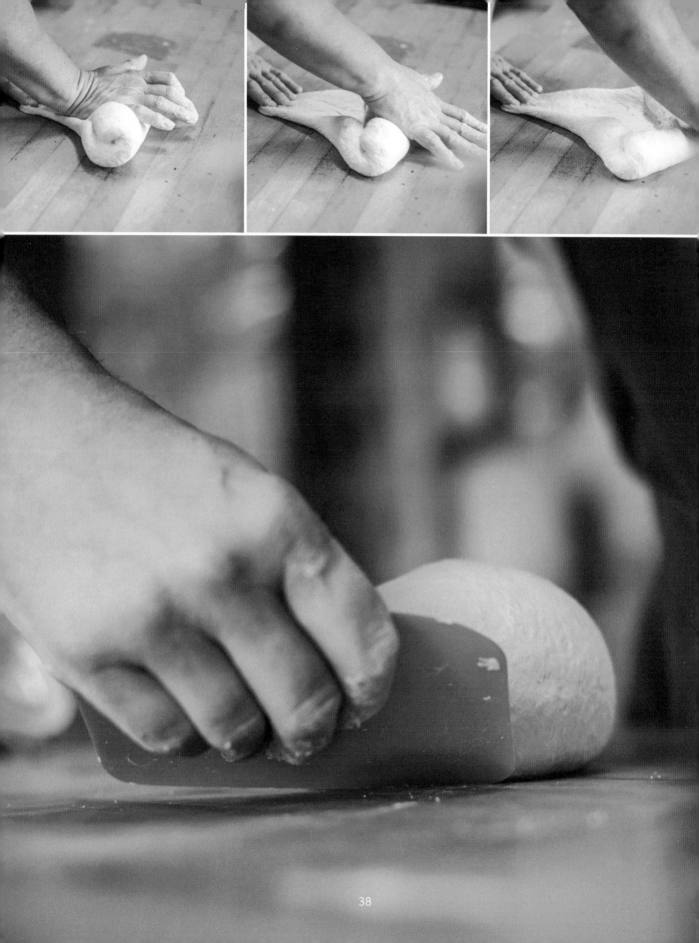

Kneading

When we knead dough we do two things:
• Homogenise the ingredients – mix everything up until it's all evenly distributed.
• Energise protein to enable the development of gluten.

The first bit is pretty straightforward; the second needs a bit of explaining. Proteins in some (but not all) flours are capable of forming gluten. Once formed, gluten makes the dough strong, elastic and capable of holding the gas produced by the yeast. Gluten forms automatically when liquid is added to the flour but will do so more readily when the dough is energised whether by hand or by a mixer.

If we want a really strong dough (flammkuchen, pitta) we use strong flour and knead it fully. Strong flour is high in gluten-making proteins and ten minutes of fairly vigorous kneading will ensure it is fully developed.

Unleavened doughs like paratha or doughs using raising agents like piadina, do not have to hold gases for a long time so only require enough kneading to homogenise the ingredients.

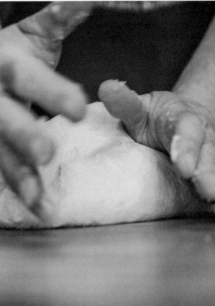

Sticky Stuff

Many of the doughs in this book will feel a little sticky when you start kneading them. Resist the temptation to add more flour. The lightest, bubbliest doughs require a softer mix with more liquid to allow the texture to open up. Protein really doesn't care if your hands and table are a mess; it just wants the energy from your hands so it can get to work making gluten.

To knead sticky doughs try using just your fingertips to lift and fold the dough. You'll be amazed at how the dough changes and develops after a short time even though you are barely touching it.

For firmer dough, this is easier to simply fold and roll the dough on your work surface.

Essentials

A bowl. We use plastic; it's light and virtually unbreakable.

A dough scraper. A simple plastic dough scraper just makes life so much easier when you're making dough.

A whisk. For whisking batter.

OUR BASIC FLATBREAD 42

FLAMMKUCHEN 44

PIADINA 46

LAHMACUN 48

NAAN BREAD 50

PITTA BREAD 52

SOCCA 54

COCA 56

CLASSIC PANCAKES 58

MSEMMEN 60

BÁNH XÈO 64

STUFFED PARATHAS 66

BREAKFAST PANCAKES 70

YORKSHIRE PUDDINGS 72

FOCCACCIA 74

KHACHAPURI 78

MANNAEESH 80

POTATO FARLS 82

SEEDED HONEY CRACKERS 84

STAFFORDSHIRE OATCAKES 86

SWEET FLATBREADS 88

FOUGASSE 92

PISSALADIÈRE 94

RYE CRISPBREADS 96

RECIPES

OUR BASIC FLATBREAD

We use this constantly for rustling up some flatbreads in the wood fired oven. You can vary the fillings to suit what you've got so really have a play with different combinations and what you've got available once you've had a practise. You don't need a lot of the flavouring – about 120g/4oz grated cheese or 60g/2oz bacon, 2 tablespoons of chopped fresh herbs or pastes. So just experiment and see what works for you.

Some flavour combinations we've used and loved -
• Mature cheddar with finely chopped flat leaf parsley
• Wild garlic with grated hard goats cheese
• Chopped fresh sage and slow cooked onion
• Black olive tapenade
• Freshly ground black pepper and a little cream cheese
• Harissa paste
• Grain mustard and finely chopped spring onions *(scallions)*
• Freshly picked fennel seeds – a favourite in late summer for their fab aniseedy flavour

- 500g · 1lb 2oz · 4 cups strong white flour
- 10g · ¼oz · 1½ tsp fine seasalt
- 5g · ⅛oz · 1¼ tsp fast acting yeast
- 330ml · 11 fl oz · 1½ cups water
- Olive oil for brushing the tops

 Oven temperature – 1 Mississippi   *Door – Off*
Between 300°C/570°F and 400°C/750°F

To make the dough

1 Mix everything together in a large bowl and then turn on to a clean work surface. Knead for 10 minutes or so until the dough is soft, smooth and springy.

2 Once the dough is fully developed, add the flavourings and carry on kneading for a couple of minutes to evenly distribute the new ingredients. Don't worry if it all gets messy again at this point.

3 Put the dough back into a clean bowl and cover. Leave the dough to rise until doubled in size and puffy.

4 Divide the dough into 8 equal pieces, shape these pieces of dough into balls, put them on to a light dusting of flour and cover with oiled clingfilm.

5 Leave them to relax and rise again for 30 minutes.

6 Roll out the dough balls to discs about 30cm/12" in diameter. Brush the tops lightly with olive oil.

7 Put them one by one on a well floured pee and then on to the oven floor.

8 Bake quickly, turning through 180 degrees for even baking. When they are done wrap them in a clean cloth to keep them warm and soft.

9 Eat as soon as possible – perfect for breakfast, brunch, lunch, dinner, supper or as a snack...

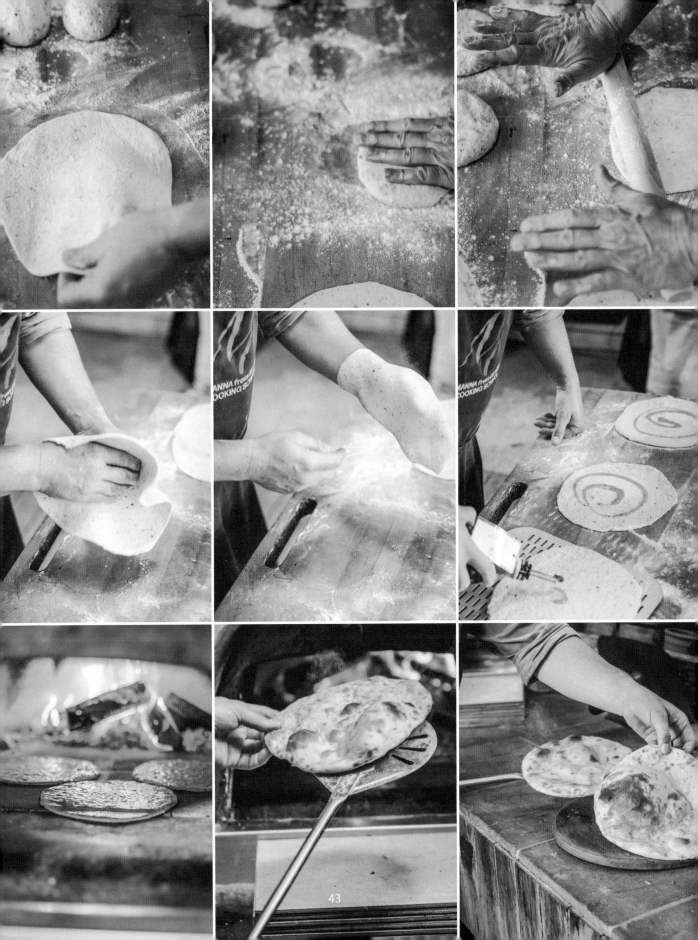

44

FLAMMKUCHEN

Flammkuchen (or Tarte Flambé if you're on the French side of the border) is a thin and delicious flatbread from the Alsace region. It is much like an Italian pizza bianca, baked at a high heat and covered with a delicious combination of crème fraîche, thinly sliced onions and bacon lardons – very simple and great for breakfast, brunch, lunch or just snacking.

This makes 2 thin flammkuchen

- 250g · 9oz · 2 cups 00 flour
- 5g · ⅛oz · ¾tsp fine sea salt
- 3g · ½₂oz · ½tsp fast acting yeast
- 15ml · ½ fl oz · 1tbsp olive oil
- 150ml · 5 fl oz · ⅝ cup warm water
- 1 medium onion *(regular or red)*, peeled and very thinly sliced
- 90g · 3oz smoked bacon lardons cut very small
- 120ml · 4 fl oz · ½ cup crème fraîche
- Salt and pepper

Oven temperature – 1 Mississippi
Between 300°C/570°F and 400°C/750°F

Door – Off

Method

1 Mix together the flour, yeast, salt, water and oil. Knead for 10 minutes to get a smooth dough. Leave in a clean bowl and cover until well risen and puffy – about 1 hour.

2 Divide the dough into two and roll out to get two 30cm/12" squares. Put one of the dough squares on to a well floured peel.

3 Spread half the crème fraîche on the top of one of the squares all the way to the edges and scatter over half the onion slices and half the bacon lardons.

4 Sprinkle over a little salt and lots of freshly ground black pepper.

5 Place the flammkuchen on to the oven floor and bake in the hot oven for 3 minutes until the base is cooked through, turning it round in the oven half way through the cooking time so the side closest the door is closer to the fire. Repeat with the other dough square and the rest of the ingredients.

6 As we said this is great for breakfast, brunch, lunch, snacks or cut into small squares and served as an appetiser with drinks.

PIADINA

Piadina are an Italian wrap from Romagna, some say the precursor to the pizza. They are unleavened so easy and quick to put together if you are running late. Originally they would be made in a large flat pan and cooked on the hob but they work even better we think on the base of your wood fired oven. Traditionaly they are made with lard. If you don't want to use lard, you can replace it with olive oil or butter.

- 250g · 9oz · 2 cups 00 flour
- 1 level teaspoon baking powder
- 5g · ⅛oz · ¾ tsp fine sea salt
- 50g · 2oz · 4 tbsp lard
- 150ml · 5fl oz · ⅝ cup cold water

Fillings -
• Parma ham
• Salami
• Mozzarella
• Dolcelatte
• Roast red or yellow peppers
• Artichoke hearts
• Olives
• Roast tomatoes
• Salad leaves and fresh herbs

 Oven temperature – 1 Mississippi   *Door – Off*
Between 300°C/570°F and 400°C/750°F

Method
1 Mix together the flour, baking powder and salt and rub in the lard.

2 Mix in the cold water and knead every-thing together to make a smooth dough.

3 Divide into 4 equal pieces and roll out on a floured surface to get a disc ½cm/¼" thick and about 25cm/10" wide.

4 Put one of the discs on a well floured peel and put on the oven floor. Repeat with the rest.

5 Bake the piadina with the door off for 3-4 minutes then take them out of the oven and cover with a clean tea towel.

6 Use as soon as possible so the piadina are super fresh and make into gorgeous soft wraps packed with your chosen fillings.

LAHMACUN

This is a meal in itself, with spicy lamb, cooked veggies and crunchy onions on top of chewy soft bread. The ground sumac adds a citrussy flavour and is easy to get hold of in good spice shops and lots of supermarkets. Lahmacuns are originally from the area around Turkey, Syria and the Lebanon and are fantastic as a brunch or lunch dish; they are also perfect for feeding a crowd at a party. This recipe will happily feed 8.

Dough -
- 450g · 1lb · 3½ cups strong white flour
- 50g · 2oz · ½ cup strong wholemeal flour
- 10g · ¼oz · 1½ tsp fine seasalt
- 5g · ⅛oz · 1¼ tsp fast acting yeast
- 30ml · 1 fl oz · 2tbsp sunflower oil
- 330ml · 11 fl oz · 1½ cups water

To serve -
- Handful of parsley *(flatleaf or curly)*, roughly chopped
- Plain yoghurt
- 2 fresh red chillies, deseeded and very finely sliced
- Salt and pepper

Filling -
• 1 large ripe tomato, roughly chopped
• 2 medium red onions, peeled
• 1 medium carrot, peeled and roughly chopped
• 1 clove garlic, peeled
• 2tbsp roughly chopped parsley
• 1 level tsp ground cumin
• 1 level tsp ground coriander
• 1 heaped tsp ground sumac
• 250g · 9oz minced lamb

Oven temperature – 1 Mississippi
Between 300°C/570°F and 400°C/750°F

Door – Off

Method

1 Mix together the flours, yeast, salt, sunflower oil and water. Knead to a smooth dough for 10 minutes and leave to rise in a clean bowl, covered, for about an hour or so until well risen and puffy.

2 Roughly chop one of the red onions and thinly slice the other. Put the roughly chopped onion in a food processor with the tomato, carrot, garlic, parsley and spices. Season well and whizz together until smooth.

3 Drain this vegetable mixture through a sieve into a bowl to get rid of some of the excess liquid. Mix the chopped vegetables with the lamb mince – it's easiest to do this by hand. You want a soft, spreadable mixture.

4 Divide the dough into eight equal pieces, roll into balls, cover with oiled clingfilm and leave to rest for 30 minutes. Then roll out each ball to a circle about 25cm/10" across. One at a time put a piece of dough on a well-

floured peel and spread an eighth of the lamb mixture over the top of the dough circle right out to the edges.

5 Shift the dough off the peel into the hot oven and cook for 2-3 minutes. A light bake should keep the base soft enough to roll without too much cracking.

6 Take the lahmacun out of the oven and put it on a board. Sprinkle some of the thinly sliced onion over the top of the cooked lamb along with some parsley, sliced chilli and a splash of yoghurt.

7 Roll the lahmacun up and serve straight away whilst you cook the rest.

NAAN BREAD

Mmmm – naan bread: puffy, warm, charred, flavourful, soft and chewy at the same time – everything we want in a flat bread. Traditionally they would be baked on the side of a tandoor but they work really well, like all our other favourites, on the base of our wood fired oven. We use ghee to brush the top of the finished naan breads to add some extra butteriness to them. Ghee is clarified butter and is used a lot in Indian cooking; you can find it in tins in most supermarkets now. We keep the naan breads wrapped up in a clean tea towel to keep them warm and soft while you are baking the rest of the batch.

For 6 naans

- 250g · 9oz · 2 cups plain *(all purpose)* flour
- 250g · 9oz · 2 cups strong white bread flour
- 10g · ¼oz · 1½ tsp fine seasalt
- 5g · ⅛oz · 1¼ tsp fast acting yeast
- 50g · 2oz · 4 tbsp softened clarified butter
  or ghee
- 250ml · 9fl oz · 1 cup 2 tbsp warm water
- 100ml · 3½ fl oz · ½ cup plain yoghurt

Oven temperature – 1 Mississippi
Between 300°C/570°F and 400°C/750°F

Door – Off

Method

1 Put the flours, yeast, salt, half the ghee and all the yoghurt into a bowl. Add the water and bring together to form a very soft dough.

2 Turn the dough on to a clean surface and knead it for 10 minutes or so until it is smooth and satiny.

3 Put the dough into a large bowl and cover. Set it aside to prove for 1-2 hours until well risen and puffy.

4 Divide the dough into 6 equal pieces and shape them into balls. Let the dough balls rest in a cool place for an hour, covered with oiled clingfilm to stop the dough sticking.

5 Moisten a patch of worktop with water and wet your hands. Shape your first dough ball into a rough teardrop about ½cm/¼" thick.

6 Brush the top of the naan with melted ghee and put it on to the oven floor using a well floured peel. No need to put the door on the oven.

7 Let the bread puff up and bake for a minute or so and while it is cooking get the next one ready. You can get into a rhythm where you are baking one, making the next, putting that in, taking the first out and shaping the 3rd.

8 When the first bread is cooked, put it into a basket and cover with a large clean cloth.

9 Eat the naans as soon as possible with your favourite lentil dhal and curries.

PITTA BREAD

Wow – these are just the best fun to make! You start with a regular dough, roll out a few thin circles and put them on the base of the hot oven floor. Then a few seconds later, boom! An inflated balloon of soft white bread ready to slash open and stuff with roast meats, salads, hummus, all manner of fillings in fact. So much better than anything you'll find in the shops. Any friends who are ambivalent about bought pitta breads will be begging you to make more when they taste these!

Makes 8 pitta breads

- 450g · 1lb · 3½ cups strong white flour
- 50g · 2oz · ½ cup wholewheat flour
- 250ml · 9 fl oz · 1 cup 2 tbsp warm water
- 100ml · 3½ fl oz · ½ cup plain yoghurt
- 10g · ¼oz · 1½ tsp fine sea salt
- 5g · ⅛oz · 1¼ tsp fast acting yeast
- 30g · 1oz · 2 tbsp nigella seeds *(optional)*

Oven temperature – 1 Mississippi
Between 300°C/570°F and 400°C/750°F

Door – Off

Method

1 Mix all the ingredients together except the nigella seeds in a large bowl to make a soft dough. Turn on to a clean work surface and knead until the dough is well developed and smooth.

2 Put the dough back into a clean bowl, cover and leave to rise for at least an hour until doubled in size.

3 Divide the dough into 8 pieces and roll each piece into an oval or circle about ½cm/¼" thick on a well floured work surface. If you want to use the nigella seeds, you can now sprinkle a few over the top of each oval and roll them well into the dough.

4 Use a small peel to place the breads on the floor of the very hot oven. They will puff up after 45 seconds or so. Flip the breads on to their other side and bake for another few seconds until they are just turning golden brown.

5 Put the cooked pittas in a basket and cover them with a clean tea towel or napkin to keep the pittas soft and supple.

6 Eat the pittas while still warm served with a little salad, garlicky hummus, crushed blackened tomatoes, finely sliced red onion and slices of grilled steak, roast lamb or chicken; in fact the filling potential is endless!

53

SOCCA  Gluten Free

These are delicious chickpea flour pancakes from the Nice and Marseilles area of southern France, traditionally cooked over charcoal in flat, wide, copper pans. Gram flour is another name for chickpea flour which is widely used in Indian and Asian cooking – it has a great nutty flavour and is gluten free. You can eat the socca with some olive oil drizzled over and some freshly ground black pepper sprinkled on top which is the traditional way but we make it into more of a meal with the addition of fresh salad leaves, chilli jam from our friends at the South Devon Chilli Farm and some cream cheese.

Makes 4 socca

- 250g · 9 oz · 2 cups gram/chickpea
  flour, sieved
- Good pinch of salt and pepper
- ½ tsp ground cumin
- 30ml · 1fl oz · 2 tbsp olive oil
- 330ml · 11fl oz · 1½ cups water
- Olive oil for frying

To serve –

- cream cheese, chilli jam and mixed
  salad leaves

*Oven temperature – 1 Mississippi
with the fire flaming*
Between 300°C/570°F and 400°C/750°F

Door – Off

Method

1 Mix the first 5 ingredients together to form a batter *(the thickness of single/pouring cream)* and leave it for 30 minutes to stand.

2 Heat a further 2tbsp of the olive oil in a wide, heavy, frying pan in the oven until the oil is really hot and just beginning to smoke.

3 Swirl around a quarter of the batter to cover the surface of the pan and cook in the oven for 3 minutes until golden brown and crispy at the edges. Halfway through cooking turn the pan 180 degrees so that both sides get equal grilling from the flames.

4 Use a flexible spatula to take the socca out of the pan and put it on a plate.

5 Spread the pancake with 1tbsp of cream cheese and 2 tsp chilli jam; put a handful of fresh salad leaves on top and then fold over the socca into a semi-circle.

6 Serve at once and continue to cook the rest of the batter in the same way.

COCA

These are a northern Spanish version of pizza but with no cheese – a lovely snack. If you happen to be in the Santa Caterina market in Barcelona, check out the bread stalls for topping ideas – spinach with onions and currants; roast peppers; slow cooked onions with olives, even peas and fresh mint.

- 500g · 1lb 2oz · 4 cups strong white flour
- 10g · ¼oz · 1½ tsp fine seasalt
- 5g · ⅛oz · 1¼ tsp fast acting yeast
- 330ml · 11 fl oz · 1½ cups water

Oven temperature – 2 Mississippi
Between 275°C/520°F and 300°C/570°F

Door – Off

Method

1 Mix the flour, water, salt and yeast together in a large bowl to make a soft dough and knead without any extra flour on a clean work surface until it is soft and springy. Put the dough into a clean bowl, cover and leave to rise until doubled in size and puffy.

2 Divide the dough into 4 equal pieces and gently shape the dough to get an oval around 25cm/10" in length.

3 Add your toppings of choice *(see right for some ideas)* and drizzle with olive oil. Season well.

4 Put the coca on to 2 well floured peels and shuffle them off the peels on to the oven floor. Bake for 5 minutes until the dough is cooked through. Serve hot or at room temperature.

Pea & Mint
Defrost 100g frozen peas and whizz until smooth in a food processor with 2tbsp chopped fresh mint and the finely grated zest of 1 lemon. Season well. Spread over the coca and drizzle with a little olive oil.

Red Pepper & Red Onion
Deseed and roughly chop 2 red peppers and whizz until smooth in a food processor with 2tbsp olive oil. Season well. Very thinly slice 1 red onion. Spread the pepper paste over the top of the coca and sprinkle over some of the red onion slices. Drizzle with a little olive oil.

Courgette and Lemon
Very thinly slice 1 large courgette (zucchini) into long ribbons – we use a vegetable peeler to do this. Toss the ribbons together with 1tsp salt and let them stand in a colander for 20 minutes to get rid of any excess moisture. Rinse and dry the courgette ribbons on some kitchen paper and arrange over the top of the coca. Very thinly slice a lemon and put some of the lemon slices on top of the courgette ribbons. Sprinkle over some freshly ground black pepper and salt and drizzle over a little olive oil.

CLASSIC PANCAKES

We love pancakes and think we should be eating them all year round, not just on Pancake Day. Pancakes cook really well in your wood fired oven – light and fluffy with crispy edges; delicious! We love our pancakes with a classic lemon and sugar topping but you can eat them with almost anything, sweet or savoury – how are you going to have yours??!

This recipe will make 12-16 pancakes
so will happily feed 6

- 250g · 9oz · 2 cups plain *(all purpose)* flour
- Pinch of salt
- 3 eggs
- 450ml · 12 fl oz · 1⅞ cups milk *(full fat or semi-skimmed, it's up to you)*
- 30g · 1oz · 2 tbsp melted butter

To serve –
- Lemon juice
- Caster sugar

Oven temperature – 2 Mississippi
Between 275°C/520°F and 300°C/570°F

Door – Off

Method

1 Put the flour and salt into a large bowl and crack in the eggs. Whisk the eggs into the flour and then whisk in the milk to get a batter the consistency of double *(heavy)* cream. Let the batter stand for 30 minutes.

2 Heat a 20cm/8" wide frying pan in the oven and add a little of the melted butter. Wipe it round the pan with some kitchen paper.

3 Add a ladleful of the batter and swirl it around the base of the pan.

4 Put the pan in the oven for 2 minutes until the pancake is golden brown on its base before flipping it over and cooking for another minute.

5 Take the pancake out of the pan and put it on a plate. Squeeze over some fresh lemon juice and sprinkle over a little caster sugar.

6 Repeat the cooking process to use up all the pancake batter and enjoy all year, not just Pancake Day!

MSEMMEN

This is a rolled and folded flat bread from Morocco, fantastic served for breakfast or brunch. The rolling and folding causes the msemmen to puff apart and crisp up to give a flaky texture created by all the layers. It sounds a complicated process but as with anything, a little practise will make everything much clearer. Check out the step-by-step photos to see what we did.

This recipe will make 4 msemmen

- 400g · 14oz · 3¼ cups 00 flour
- 150g · 5oz · 1¼ cups extra fine semolina
- 15g · ½ oz · 1tbsp caster sugar
- 10g · ¼oz · 1½ tsp fine seasalt
- 5g · ⅛oz · 1¼ tsp fast acting yeast
- 330ml · 11 fl oz · 1½ cups warm water
- 150ml · 5 fl oz · 3½ tbsp sunflower oil

 Oven temperature – 2 Mississippi　　　*Door – Off*
Between 275°C/520°F and 300°C/570°F

Method

1 Mix together the flour and 100g of the semolina with the sugar, yeast and salt. Add the water to make a soft dough. Knead until the dough is smooth and elastic.

2 Put the dough in a clean bowl, cover it and leave to rise for at least 45 minutes until doubled in size and puffy.

3 Divide the dough into 8 equal pieces and shape each piece into a ball.

4 Use a rolling pin to roll out the dough balls into very thin circles about 30cm/12" in diameter. You should be almost able to see through the dough it is that thin.

5 Brush the circle with some of the sunflower oil and sprinkle over a little of the remaining semolina. Fold 2 sides into the middle to form a rectangle, brush the top with more oil and sprinkle over more semolina and fold in the 2 ends to make a square.

6 Roll out the second ball of dough to get a large thin circle as you did with the first.

Brush with more oil and sprinkle with a little more semolina. Put the first dough square into the middle of the second dough circle and fold the two sides in to make a rectangle again. Brush with oil and sprinkle with semolina and fold in the ends to make another square.

7 Roll out the dough square to get a square 20cm/8" across.

8 Use a well floured peel to put the msemmen on to the oven floor and bake for 2½-3 minutes on each side until golden brown.

9 While the first msemmen is cooking, repeat the rolling, oiling, sprinkling and folding process with the next 2 balls of dough to get another square to roll out. You should end up with 4 msemmen.

10 When the msemmen are cooked, keep them warm and serve as a breakfast or brunch dish with fresh fruit, yoghurt and honey.

BÁNH XÈO  Gluten Free

We first came across these delicious stuffed pancakes in a market in coastal Hoi An in Vietnam. The lady running the stall had a massive vat of the pancake batter and about 8 gas burners to cook them on. She started first thing in the morning and made the bánh xèo for breakfast for tourists and workers alike, churning them out until the batter was gone. Then she packed up and headed home for the day. To be honest they were so good she wasn't there much after 10.30am.

When you find something you love on your travels it can be a bit of a worry trying to recreate them at home but these bánh xèo work really well, especially in a wood fired oven and the ingredients used are all easy to get hold of. They are great for breakfast or brunch but work well at any time of the day.

This recipe will make 8 pancakes 15cm/6" in diameter

- 225g · 8oz · 1⅖ cups rice flour
- 30g · 1oz · 2tbsp cornflour (cornstarch)
- ½ tsp ground turmeric
- ½ tsp salt
- 300ml · ½ pint · 1¼ cups water
- 100ml · 3½ fl oz · 7 tbsp coconut milk

Oven temperature – 2 Mississippi with the fire flaming
Between 275°C/520°F and 300°C/570°F

- 120g · 4oz cooked prawns
- 150g · 5oz button mushrooms, finely sliced
- 6 spring onions (scallions), very thinly sliced
- 2 cloves garlic, peeled and crushed
- 200g · 7oz bean sprouts
- Sunflower oil for frying
- 4 large handfuls shredded iceberg lettuce or Chinese leaf mixed with ½ handful each roughly chopped fresh coriander and freshly chopped mint

Door – Off

Method

1 Mix together the rice flour, cornflour, ground turmeric and salt and stir in the water and coconut milk to get a smooth batter. Leave the batter to stand for 30 minutes.

2 Mix all the mushrooms with 2tbsp of the sunflower oil and cook in a small frying pan in the oven until the mushrooms are golden brown. Stir in the spring onions and garlic and turn all of them into a clean bowl.

3 Put a 15cm/6" frying pan in the oven to heat through for a couple of minutes and add 1tbsp sunflower oil.

4 Add ⅛ of the batter and swirl around the base of the pan. Put it into the oven and let the pancake cook for 2 minutes. Add ⅛ of the mushroom mixture to the surface of the

pancake and put the pan back in the oven for another 2-3 minutes.

5 30 seconds before the pancake is ready, sprinkle over ⅛ of the bean sprouts and ⅛ of the prawns. Using a flexible spatula take the bánh xèo out of the pan. The pancake will come away from the base of the pan when it's ready so don't panic if it's sticking a little; just cook it until it comes away from the base on its own.

6 Put a handful of the leafy mixture on top of the bean sprouts and fold the bánh xèo in half.

7 Serve at once with a little chilli dipping sauce and carry on cooking the rest of the mixture and using the rest of the ingredients until you've made another 7 bánh xèo.

STUFFED PARATHAS

We had stuffed paratha regularly for breakfast on our travels round Rajasthan in Northern India. Served with mango chutney, lime pickle and yoghurt it was a great start to the day. You can serve it as an accompaniment to an Indian meal or with some simply grilled meat. In India they were cooked over open fires using discs of dried cow dung as fuel but they work just as well in your wood fired oven. You can also vary the filling – we had them with sweet potato, pumpkin, even wilted spinach.

This recipe will make 4 stuffed parathas

- 150g · 5oz · 1¼ cups plain *(all purpose)* flour
- 50g · 2oz · ½ cup wholemeal flour
- ½ tsp fine sea salt
- 30ml · 1 fl oz · 2tbsp sunflower oil
- Around 100ml · 3½ fl oz · ½ cup warm water
- Extra ghee or butter and oil to cook the paratha

- 1 fresh green chilli, deseeded if you like and finely chopped
- 1 medium onion, peeled and finely chopped
- 1 level tsp ground coriander
- 1 level tsp ground cumin
- ½ tsp ground turmeric
- 150g · 5oz floury potatoes, peeled, boiled and mashed
- 5g · ½ tsp fine sea salt
- 15ml · ½ fl oz · 1tbsp sunflower oil
- Handful fresh coriander, chopped very finely
- Melted butter or ghee

Oven temperature – 2 Mississippi with the fire flaming
Between 275°C/520°F and 300°C/570°F

Door – Off

Method

1 To make the filling, heat the oil in a large heavy pan in the wood fired oven. Add the chilli and onion and cook them gently for 4-5 minutes or until they are soft. Add the ground coriander, cumin and turmeric and fry for another 2 minutes. Stir this onion mixture into the mashed potato with the chopped fresh coriander and season well with salt.

2 To make the dough, put the flours and salt into a large bowl and add the oil. Stirring with a spoon or a dough scraper, slowly mix in enough of the warm water for you to be able to form a fairly firm dough.

3 Knead the dough on a clean work surface until you get a soft and smooth, non-sticky dough. If it's sticky, add a little bit more flour and continue to bind.

4 Cut the dough into 4 equal pieces and shape into balls. Divide the potato mixture into 4 equal pieces and shape them into balls as well. If the mixture is sticky put some flour on your hands to stop it sticking.

5 Roll the dough balls out to about 15cm/6" in diameter and place the potato balls on top of each disc of dough.

6 Using your thumbs and forefingers, pinch the dough closed around the filling until the filling is fully enclosed with no gaps or holes. Gently flatten the paratha using the palm of your hand and dust them with flour on both sides.

7 Roll the parathas out on a floured surface until they are ½cm/ ¼" thick.

8 Heat 1tbsp ghee or butter in a frying pan in the oven and carefully slide in the parathas, cooking one at a time. Cook them on both sides until golden brown all over and rotate the pan during cooking so each side of the paratha gets an even burst of the flames.

9 Brush a little more melted ghee on to the finished parathas and keep the cooked ones warm whilst you cook the rest. Serve at once with a curry or some pickles and yoghurt.

American Style ★ BREAKFAST PANCAKES

These make a great breakfast or brunch and are a sure fire winner when we've got children staying – they particularly love them with crispy bacon, banana slices and maple syrup drizzled over the top – or is that just us??!!

- 150g · 5oz · 1¼ cups plain (all purpose) flour
- 1 level tsp baking powder
- ½ tsp fine seasalt
- 30g · 1oz · 2tbsp caster sugar
- 220ml · 8fl oz · 1cup milk
- 2 eggs, separated
- 30g · 1oz · 2tbsp melted butter

Oven temperature – 3 Mississippi
Between 250°C/480°F and 275°C/520°F

Door – Off

Method

1 Mix the flour, baking powder, salt and sugar in a large bowl and whisk in the milk, egg yolks and melted butter to get a smooth thick batter.

2 Whisk the egg whites until they are at the soft peak stage and fold them into the batter.

3 Put a large frying pan or a smooth griddle in the oven and let it heat up.

4 Add a small piece of butter and wipe it around the surface of the pan. Add a large spoonful of the batter to form a pancake about 10cm/4" wide to one side of the pan. Add another spoonful of batter so you're cooking 2 pancakes at once.

5 Once little bubbles start forming on the top of the pancakes, flip them over and cook until the other side is golden brown and the pancakes have puffed up.

6 Take them out of the pan and keep them warm while you cook the rest of the batter in the same way. Wipe the pan out with a little extra melted butter on some kitchen paper before every batch of pancakes.

7 Serve with berries, yoghurt and honey or with thin, crispy bacon and maple syrup for a fab breakfast or brunch.

YORKSHIRE PUDDINGS

Yorkshire Puddings are an irreplaceable part of the great British Roast Beef dinner, traditionally served before the meat to fill you up and make sure the beef went further. In recent years they have become much more than that – now they are regularly seen on pub menus stuffed with sausages and onion gravy and at swanky parties served as mini puds and filled with rare roast beef and mustard or horseradish cream; the Yorkshire pud is for everyone! What is crucial in the cooking is a hot oven and we can guarantee that in the wood fired oven. If you cook your Yorkshires in your wood fired oven from now on, you'll be the envy of all your friends – crisp light and puffy; pudding perfection!

Makes 12 individual Yorkshire puddings

- 250g · 9oz · 2 cups plain *(all purpose)* flour
- 150ml · 5 fl oz · ⅝ cup milk
- 150ml · 5 fl oz · ⅝ cup water
- 4 eggs
- Pinch of salt
- 2tbsp sunflower oil

 Oven temperature – 3 Mississippi
Between 250°C/480°F and 275°C/520°F

Door – Ajar

Method

1 Sift the flour and salt into a large bowl. Crack the eggs into the flour and pour in half the milk. Whisk all this together and then gradually stir in the rest of the milk and all the water to make a smooth batter. Leave the batter to stand for 30 minutes.

2 Wipe a 12 hole muffin tray with the oil using a piece of kitchen paper and put the tray in the oven to heat up for 2-3 minutes.

3 Put the batter in a jug and pour it evenly into the muffin holes as quickly as you can so the tray doesn't get cold.

4 Put the tray back in the oven and cover the entrance with the door, leaving it ajar.

5 Bake the puddings for 6 minutes and then quickly turn the tray round so the front is at the back. Make sure you wear your heat-proof gauntlets when you do this.

6 Cook the puddings for another 5-6 minutes with the door ajar until they are well risen and golden brown.

7 Take them out of the oven and serve at once.

FOCCACCIA

This is one of the most popular breads on our village bread box delivery and known in some friends' house by the kids as David's bread; the dough is a bit challenging to make as it's so soft but it forms this incredibly big pillow that gives a satisfying wobble when patted and you can just imagine sinking into it for an afternoon nap; well maybe... The recipe uses a biga which is a pre-ferment made in advance to add flavour and texture to the dough so you need to plan ahead if you're going to make some foccaccias – but you'll be glad you did!

For the Biga -
- 250g · 9 oz · 2 cups 00 flour
- 250ml · 9 fl oz · 1 cup 2 tbsp room temperature water
- 1g · ¼ tsp fast acting yeast

☆ *To make the biga mix the flour, water and yeast to make a wet batter. Cover and leave overnight or up to 36 hours.*

For the Dough -
- All the biga
- 500g · 1lb 2oz · 4 cups 00 flour
- 60ml · 2 fl oz · 4 tbsp olive oil
- 5g · ⅛oz · 1¼ tsp fast acting yeast
- 15g · ½oz · 1½ tsp fine sea salt
- 275ml · 10 fl oz · 1¼ cups water

For the topping -
- 10 cherry tomatoes, halved
- 2 medium red onions, peeled and very finely sliced
- A handful of fresh marjoram or a level tsp of mixed dried herbs
- 30ml · 1 fl oz · 2 tbsp extra virgin olive oil
- Coarse sea salt

Oven temperature – 3 Mississippi
Between 250°C/480°F and 275°C/520°F

Door – Ajar

To make the dough

1 Mix the yeast, flour, salt, 1tbsp of the oil and the water with the biga. Mix to a soft, sticky dough.

2 Knead the dough on a clean surface for about 5 minutes. The dough will be very sticky but resist the temptation to add more flour; this wet dough will give a fabulous bubbly texture to your final bread. To knead the dough, it's easier if you continuously lift it off the table with your finger tips, stretching it towards you and folding it back over itself. Try not to break through the outer surface of the dough as then it will become very messy – this sounds complicated but it's just practise and worth the mess as it does make amazing foccaccia.

3 Tip the remaining olive oil in to a shallow tray. Place the dough in the oil. Cover the dough and leave for 1 hour to rise.

4 Oil a patch of your work top and gently tip the dough on to it. Using the tips of your fingers, dimple the surface of the dough and ease it gently into a rectangle about 30x25cm/12x10".

5 Scatter the tomato halves across the dough and press each one firmly down into the dough. Cover the dough again and leave for 15 minutes.

6 After 15 minutes dimple the dough again and press each piece of tomato further into the dough. Leave it for another 10 minutes.

7 Press any tomatoes that are making a bid for freedom back into the dough and sprinkle on the herbs. Toss the onions in the 2tbsp oil and spread these over the dough then sprinkle generously with some coarse seasalt.

8 Using a well floured peel, put the bread on the oven floor and put the door on so it's ajar. Bake the foccaccia until the upper surface is a good golden brown. If the bread is browning too quickly, put a deep roasting tin over the top to protect it. The loaf should take about 15 minutes to bake - the foccaccia will be golden brown and firm on top but still springy inside.

☆ *We could make a very nice foccaccia without the overnight ferment, in a couple of hours and without all the prior work involved in this recipe. So why don't we ... ?*

... Because whilst that one without the biga will be good, this one, with a little practice, will be the best foccaccia you'll ever make.

Trust me!

KHACHAPURI

These are fun to make and very filling, great for feeding a hungry crowd – and good for breakfast and brunch. We mix three cheeses, mozzarella for stringiness, mature Cheddar for sharpness and feta for saltiness. Nothing like the original Georgian mixture but let's not allow a lack of authenticity to get in the way of a good snack.

This recipe will make 4 khachapuri
- 500g · 1lb 2oz · 4 cups strong white flour
- 10g · ¼oz · 1½ tsp fine seasalt
- 5g · ⅛oz · 1¼ tsp fast acting yeast
- 330ml · 11 fl oz · 1½ cups room temperature water
- 120g · 4oz · 1 cup mozzarella, ripped into little pieces
- 120g · 4oz · 1 cup grated mature Cheddar
- 120g · 4oz · 1 cup crumbled feta
- 4 medium eggs
- Olive oil
- 2tsp chopped fresh thyme or 1tsp dried thyme

 Oven temperature – 3 Mississippi
Between 250°C/480°F and 275°C/520°F

Door – Ajar

Method

1 Mix the flour, salt and yeast together in a large bowl. Add the water and mix well. Knead the dough on a clean work surface until smooth and springy.

2 Put the dough back in a clean bowl, cover and leave to rise for 2 hours.

3 Mix the three cheeses with the thyme and oil and leave in the fridge.

4 Divide the dough into 4 even pieces. Shape into balls, cover with oiled clingfilm and leave to rest for 30 minutes. This will make shaping the breads much easier.

5 Take a ball of dough and place it on a lightly floured work surface. Sprinkle a little flour on top.

6 Use your fingertips to press the dough out to make an oval about 22x10cm/9x4".

7 Take two corners at one of the ends and cross one over the other. Press down to create the bow of your boat-shaped khachapuri. Repeat at the other end to make the stern.

8 Roll the edges in and press down to make the sides of your boat. You should now have a nice, deep pocket to fill with cheese.

9 Repeat the shaping process with the other 3 dough balls.

10 Divide the cheese mixture between the 4 khachapuri.

11 Put 2 of the khachapuri on to a well floured peel and shuffle them on to your oven floor. Repeat with the other 2 khachapuri.

12 Bake for 5 minutes. Then make a hollow in the cheese fillings – be careful they will be hot – and crack an egg into each khachapuri. Put them back in the oven for another 5 minutes until cooked. The sides and the ends should be well risen, golden brown and puffy, the cheeses bubbly and browned and the eggs still runny.

MANNAEESH

These are delicious puffy flat breads from the Lebanon laden with za'atar, a gorgeous mix of sesame seeds and aromatic herbs – mint, marjoram and thyme. We like to make our own as we have a garden full of herbs that need using but you can use ready-made za'atar - that's fine too! Use the Mannaeesh for dunking in great olive oil and dukkah, in dips or eating with salads and soups. The yoghurt gives a lovely softness to the crumb as well as a slight tang to the taste. Literally everything stops the day we bake these as they are so good they get ripped into while they are still hot!

Makes 3 mannaeesh

For the bread -
- 500g · 1lb 2oz · 4 cups 00 flour
- 10g · ¼oz · 1½ tsp fine sea salt
- 5g · ⅛oz · 1¼ tsp fast acting yeast
- 100ml · 3 ½ fl oz · ½ cup yoghurt
- 200ml · 7 fl oz · ⅞ cup warm water
- 30ml · 1 fl oz · 2 tbsp olive oil

For the za'atar –
- 1tbsp each finely chopped fresh mint, marjoram, thyme and sesame seeds
- 1 level tsp ground sumac
- 1 level tsp fine sea salt
- 45ml · 1½ fl oz · 3tbsp olive oil

Oven temperature – 3 Mississippi
Between 250°C/480°F and 275°C/520°F

Door – Ajar

Method

1 In a large bowl, mix together all the ingredients for the bread. Form into a soft dough and knead well on a tabletop until smooth and elastic.

2 Put the dough in a large, clean bowl, cover and leave to rise until doubled in size.

3 Mix all the za'atar ingredients together.

4 Split the dough into 3 equal pieces and roll out into discs 12.5cm/5" in diameter.

5 Leave the discs covered with a clean tea towel on a floured work surface for 20 minutes to puff back up.

6 Put the dough circles on a well floured peel and use a dough scraper or a butter knife to create a lattice on the top of the dough. Divide the za'atar equally between the dough circles and sprinkle over the surface, pressing down gently so the seeds don't ping off.

7 Use the peel to put them in a hot oven and bake for 5-6 minutes until the bread is cooked through but still soft and white.

8 Cool on a wire rack and serve as soon as you can.

POTATO FARLS

These Irish potato breads are a great accompaniment for breakfasts or brunch which is how we enjoy ours. We play a game with an Irish friend when we say what we can't imagine life without – we say bread and he says potatoes (yes I know, we make our own entertainment...). Well here's the perfect combination of the two and a great way of using up some leftover mashed potatoes.

Makes 8 farls

- 450g · 1lb · 4 cups cooked and mashed floury potatoes
- 50g · 2oz · 4 tbsp butter, softened
- 100g · 3½oz · ⅘ cup plain *(all purpose)* flour, plus extra for rolling out
- ¼ tsp baking powder
- Salt and black pepper
- Extra butter, for cooking

 Oven temperature – 3 Mississippi   *Door – Off*
Between 250°C/480°F and 275°C/520°F

Method

1 Add the butter to the potatoes and mash until smooth.

2 Sift the flour with the baking powder over the potato mix and combine well – this is easiest to do with your hands. Taste for seasoning and adjust, if required.

3 The mixture should make a smooth dough. You can add more flour if the mixture is too wet and a little milk if it is too dry.

4 Divide the dough into two halves. Form one piece into a ball, then pat it out on a floured surface into a rough circle with a diameter of about 15 cm/6" and a thickness of 1cm/½".

5 Pop a shallow frying pan into the oven and warm it through. Add a little butter and use a brush to spread it round the pan. Transfer the first circle of dough into the pan. Use a dough scraper to mark four

quarters into the dough but don't cut all the way through.

6 Cook for around 5 minutes in the oven with the door off until the farls are golden brown on the base. Flip the farl over and cook on the other side for another 3 or 4 minutes. Remove to a warm plate.

7 Repeat the process with the other half of the dough mix.

8 These are great for breakfasts or brunches so serve with some roast tomatoes, crispy bacon, fried eggs – all done in the wood fired oven of course! Also delicious as a supper dish with some Boston baked beans and slow roast pork.

SEEDED HONEY CRACKERS

A delicious crisp bread inspired by one of Holly's trips to London when she and her great friend Meg headed to Ottolenghi in Islington for lunch. This is our take on the pack of gorgeously snappy and seedy crispbreads she brought back to Devon. The recipe will make a lot of crackers so keep them in a big tin and break off bits to snack on or to have with cheese and preserves.

- 250g · 9oz · 2 cups strong white flour
- 5g · ⅛oz · ¾ tsp fine sea salt
- 3g · ½0oz · ½ tsp fast acting yeast
- 165ml · 5½ fl oz · ¾ cup warm water
- 50g · 2oz · 2tbsp runny honey
- 30g · 1oz · 2tbsp each poppy seeds, sesame seeds, sunflower seeds and flaked almonds
- 15g · ½oz · 1tbsp fennel seeds

Oven temperature – 3 Mississippi
Between 250°C/480°F and 275°C/520°F

Door – Off

Method

1 Mix together the flour, yeast, salt and water in a large bowl.

2 Turn the mixture on to a clean work surface and knead well for 5 minutes to get a smooth, soft dough.

3 Put the dough back into a clean bowl and leave covered until well risen and puffy – about 1 hour.

4 Mix the seeds and almonds together. Thin the honey by mixing in 1tbsp boiling water.

5 Cut the dough into 50g/2oz pieces and shape each one into a ball.

6 On a floured surface, roll the balls into a very thin circle about 25cm/10" in diameter and put the first one on to a well floured peel.

7 Brush the top of the dough circle on the peel with some of the diluted honey and

sprinkle over 1tbsp of the seed mixture.

8 Cook for 2-3 minutes until the dough is cooked through but not browning too much otherwise the seeds and almonds will go bitter.

9 Take the bread out of the oven using a peel and place on a wire rack to cool and crisp up.

10 Repeat until all the dough, honey and seeds are used up.

STAFFORDSHIRE OATCAKES

Our brother-in-law Dave grew up in Staffordshire and whenever he goes back to see his mum, he raves about the Staffordshire oatcakes. More like a thick oaty crepe than the small crisp Scottish oatcakes, they are served for breakfast with bacon and cheese.

Makes 12 oatcakes

- 250g · 9oz · 2 cups fine oatmeal
- 150g · 5oz · 1¼ cups plain *(all purpose)* flour
- 150g · 5oz · 1¼ cups wholemeal flour
- 10g · ¼oz · 1½ tsp fine seasalt
- 5g · ⅛oz · 1¼ tsp fast acting yeast
- 500ml · 18 fl oz · 2¼ cups milk
- 500ml · 18 fl oz · 2¼ cups water
- 30ml · 1 fl oz · 2tbsp sunflower oil

 Oven temperature – 3 Mississippi   *Door – Off*
Between 250°C/480°F and 275°C/520°F

Method

1 Put the oatmeal, flour, salt and yeast in a large bowl and mix well. Stir in the milk and water gradually to make a batter that looks like double *(heavy)* cream. Beat well to combine everything and to start the yeast working.

2 Cover the bowl and leave for 2 hours until the batter is thick but frothy.

3 When you're ready to cook, put a large frying pan in the oven and heat it through.

4 Wipe out the pan with a little of the sunflower oil using a piece of kitchen paper.

5 Swirl in a ladleful of the batter and cook the oatcake for a minute on each side until golden brown.

6 Take the oatcake out of the pan and keep warm while you make the rest of the batter into oatcakes.

7 While you're cooking the oatcakes, put a roasting tin of bacon slices alongside the pan in the oven and cook through. Keep them warm too.

8 Serve the oatcakes with a few rashers of bacon on each one and some grated Cheddar cheese sprinkled over. Keep the loaded oatcakes in the oven for a couple of minutes until the cheese has melted and serve at once with a big mug of tea.

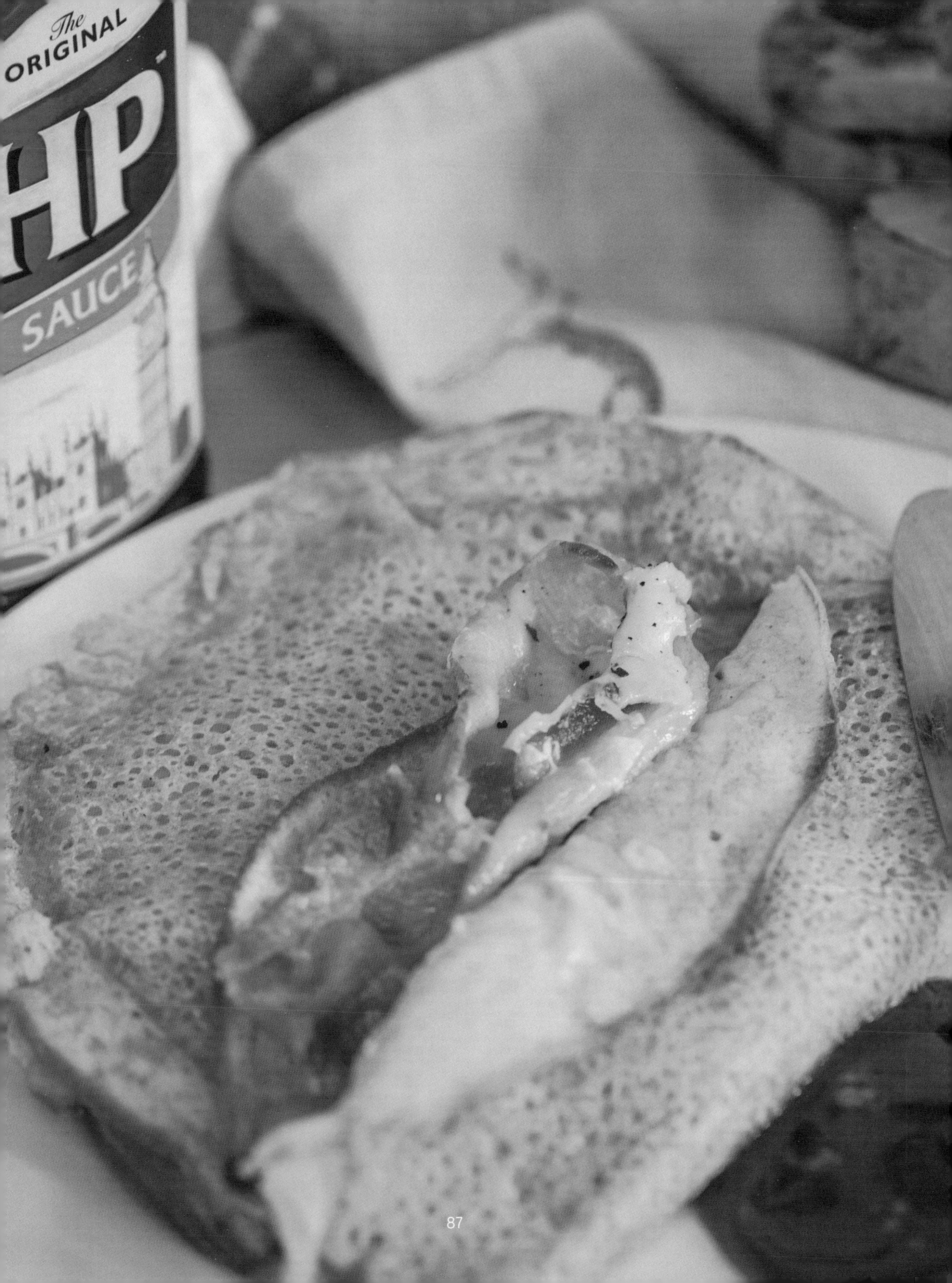
The ORIGINAL
HP
SAUCE

SWEET FLATBREADS

Lots of people think savoury when they hear flatbreads but you can make some fantastic sweet ones too. Here are 2 classics - apple & cinnamon and banana, chocolate and hazelnut. Real winners! Each flat bread will serve 8-10 happily – serve warm with some vanilla icecream. Delicious!

- 500g · 1lb 2oz · 4 cups strong white flour
- 150ml · 5fl oz · ½ cup & 2tbsp warm water
- 120ml · 4fl oz · ½ cup milk
- 1 egg
- 30g · 1oz · 2tbsp butter
- 30g · 1oz · 2tbsp caster sugar
- 10g · ¼oz · 1½ tsp fine seasalt
- 5g · ⅛oz · 1¼ tsp fast acting yeast

Apple & Cinnamon -
- 3 eating apples
- 50g · 2oz · scant ½ cup icing
  (confectioner's) sugar
- ½ tsp ground cinnamon

Chocolate, Banana & Hazelnut -
- 2 medium bananas
- 150g · 5oz milk chocolate
- 50g · 2fl oz · ¼ cup double *(heavy)* cream
- 50g · 2oz · ½ cup hazelnuts, roughly
  chopped or bashed in a pestle & mortar

Oven temperature – 3 Mississippi
Between 250°C/480°F and 275°C/520°F

Door – Off

Method

1 Mix together the flour, water, milk, egg, butter, caster sugar, yeast and salt. Knead to get a smooth soft dough. Leave covered to rise in a warm place for about an hour or until doubled in size and puffy.

2 Split the dough into 2 equal pieces and roll each one out on a lightly floured surface to get a rectangle about 25x30cm/10x12 inches.

For the Apple Flatbread

1 Core the apples and slice them very thinly, leaving the skin on. Arrange the slices over the top of the dough.

2 Bake for 10 minutes turning from time to time to get an even bake. When it's cooked take the flatbread out of the oven and let it cool on a cooling rack.

3 Mix the cinnamon with the icing (confectioner's) sugar and the smallest amount of water to get a thick icing.

4 Take the apple flat bread out of the oven and let it cool for 10 minutes before drizzling the cinnamon icing over the top.

For the Banana, Chocolate & Hazelnut Flatbread

1 Melt the chocolate and cream together in a heavy saucepan near the oven door and mix together with a spatula. Spread the chocolate mixture over the top of one of the rectangles. Peel and slice the bananas and arrange them over the top of the chocolate spread.

2 Bake the flat bread in the oven for 5 minutes, turning from time to time to get an even bake. After the 5 minutes, sprinkle over the hazelnuts and return to the oven for another 5 minutes. Take the flat bread out of the oven and let it cool on a wire rack for 5 minutes before chopping into pieces and serving warm.

FOUGASSE

Fougasses are flat breads made with an olive oil dough from the south of France; we love seeing them stacked up in the Provencal markets and boulangeries ready to take away. They come in different shapes – palm leaves, wheat ears or ladders but however they are shaped, they just taste great!

Makes 4 fougasse

- 500g · 1lb 2oz · 4 cups strong white flour
- 3tbsp olive oil
- 10g · ¼oz · 1½ tsp fine sea salt
- 5g · ⅛oz · 1¼ tsp fast acting yeast
- 300ml · 10 fl oz · 1¼ cups room temp-erature water

- 1 large onion, peeled and finely chopped
- 1 heaped tbsp chopped fresh sage
- 2 tbsp olive oil
- 200g · 7oz bacon lardons
- 150g · 5oz · 1½ cups grated Gruyere or Cheddar cheese
- Salt and pepper

 You can vary the fillings to use other ingredients such as chopped olives, sun-dried tomatoes, chopped fresh rosemary or just leave it plain.

☆ *As you can see we didn't use a peel for the fougasses but a baking sheet covered with baking parchment as we didn't have a peel big enough for 2 of them. Shoot the fougasses off the baking sheet as you would do normally but put the baking parchment in the oven with them. Then you can pull on the paper to get them out when they are cooked which definitely helps get them out!*

🔥 *Oven temperature – 3 Mississippi*
Between 250°C/480°F and 275°C/520°F

Door – Ajar

Method

1 In a large bowl, mix the flour, the 3tbsp olive oil, salt and yeast together with the water until it all comes together. Turn on to a clean work surface and knead the dough until it is smooth and springy.

2 Put the dough back in to a clean bowl, cover and leave to rise for 1½ hours until well-risen and puffy.

3 While the dough is rising, you can cook the onion. Mix the finely chopped onion with the sage and the 2tbsp olive oil and a pinch of salt and pepper. Put this mixture in a small heavy frying pan and cook it gently in the oven until the onion is soft and golden, stirring the mixture from time to time. This will take about 10 minutes. When it's done, put the sage and onion into a bowl to cool down.

4 Put the bacon lardons in a clean frying pan in the oven until cooked through and starting to crisp up. You don't need to add any oil to them as the bacon fat will come out while they are cooking. Add them to the onion mixture and mix together.

5 When the dough has risen, turn it on to the work surface again and flatten it out. Add the cooled onion and bacon mixture and knead it into the dough.

6 Divide the dough into 4 equal pieces and shape into balls. Cover with lightly oiled clingfilm and leave the dough balls to rise again for 30 minutes.

7 When they have risen back up again, roll the dough balls out to ovals about 25cm/10" long and about 12.5cm/5" wide.

8 Sprinkle the grated cheese over half of each one and then fold the non-cheesy half on top of the cheesy half. Use your finger-tips to press down into the dough joining the top to the bottom.

9 Leave the pieces of dough to rest again under lightly oiled clingfilm for another 10 minutes and then roll them out on a lightly floured surface to get a half oval shape again about 20cm/10" long.

10 Use a blunt knife or a dough scraper to cut through the dough to make 7 slits in each piece, each about 7.5cm/3" long, fanning around from one side to the other. You still want 4 pieces of dough, each with 7 slits in it so make sure you don't cut through the edges.

11 Brush the top of each fougasse with a little extra olive oil and put them, one at a time, on to a well-floured peel. Put the fougasses on to the clean oven floor (*at 3 Mississippi*) and cover the entrance with the door so that it's just ajar.

12 Cook for 8-10 minutes until the flat-breads are golden brown and cooked through. Take them out of the oven and cool on a wire rack. Serve warm or at room temperature, ripped into pieces – they are great for serving with cheese, soup or just dunking into some more good olive oil with some dukkah or seeds.

PISSALADIÈRE

Imagine sitting on a sun-drenched terrace overlooking the glistening Mediterranean, a glass of chilled rosé in hand and contentedly chomping on the utter deliciousness that is pissaladière - sweet and very slow-cooked onions topped with salty anchovies and olives baked on an olive oil dough; this has to be one of our all time favourite salty snacks even if most of the time we're eating it on the slightly less sunny Devon coast.

- 500g · 1lb 2oz · 4 cups strong white flour
- 10g · ¼oz · 1½ tsp fine seasalt
- 5g · ⅛oz · 1¼ tsp fast acting yeast
- 60ml · 2 fl oz · 4tbsp olive oil
- 275ml · 10fl oz · 1¼ cups warm water
- 5 large onions, peeled and very thinly sliced
- 1tsp dried thyme
- 2 x 100g · 3½oz jars or tins anchovies
- 30 pitted olives, black or green

 Oven temperature – 4 Mississippi
Between 220°C/430°F and 250°C/480°F

Door – Ajar

Method

1 Mix together the flour, yeast, salt, water and 1tbsp of the oil. Knead for 5 minutes to get a smooth dough. Leave in a clean bowl with a cover on until well risen and puffy – about 1 hour or so.

2 While the dough is rising, heat the rest of the oil in a large wide pan and add the onions and dried thyme with a good pinch of salt. Cook in the oven in a large uncovered pan until the onions have halved in volume and are completely soft and golden. Drain through a sieve.

3 Drain the anchovies and cut the fillets in half lengthways. Cut the pitted olives in half lengthways too.

4 Cut the dough into 2 equal pieces and roll them out to get 2 rectangles about 30x25cm/12x10". Put the dough on a well floured board.

5 Put the onions on the dough rectangles and spread them right to the edges.

6 Make a lattice pattern over the top of the onions with the anchovy strips and put the olives in the centre of the anchovy diamonds.

7 Shuffle each pissaladière on to a well floured peel and use it to put them on to the oven floor. Bake the pissaladières in the oven for 12-15 minutes until the dough is cooked through with the door closed.

8 When the pissaladières are cooked, take them out of the oven using a metal peel and leave on a cooling rack for a few minutes.

9 Cut into pieces and serve warm with salad for a light lunch or cut into small squares with drinks as an appetiser.

☆ *Alternative – if you really don't like anchovies, you can use strips of roasted, skinned red peppers instead which give the pissaladière added sweetness on top of the onions instead of the anchovies' saltiness but honestly the anchovies are unbeatable!*

RYE CRISPBREADS

These are delicious Scandinavian-style crisp breads with a gorgeous nutty flavour from the rye flour and a superlative snap! Make a big batch as they keep really well in an airtight tin; well they would do if they weren't so delicious to snack on! The gluten in rye flour doesn't need to be kneaded so that's another bonus!

The crispbreads are great served with cheese or ham and pickles as well as smoked and cured fish. The dough this recipe makes is quite sticky but bear with it as it does make fantastic flatbreads.

Makes 12 crispbreads

- 400g · 14oz · 3¼ cups light rye flour
- 10g · ¼oz · 1½ tsp fine sea salt
- 5g · ⅛ oz · 1½ tsp fast acting yeast
- 300ml · 10 fl oz · 1¼ cup warm water
- 30g · 1oz · 2tbsp golden linseed
- 10g · 1tsp crushed fennel seeds *(optional)*

Oven temperature – 5 Mississippi
Between 175°C/350°F and 220°C/430°F

Door – Ajar

Method

1 Mix the flour in a large mixing bowl with the linseed, salt and yeast and the crushed fennel seeds if you are using them.

2 Stir the water into the flour mixture to make a sticky dough – don't be tempted to add more flour!

3 Cover the bowl and leave the dough to puff up for an hour or so.

4 Divide the dough into 12 pieces and roll into balls. Roll out the dough balls on a well floured surface until you get thin circles about 20cm/8" wide.

5 Prick the dough with a fork to let out any moisture from the dough. Use a well-floured peel to put each disc on the base of the oven and bake until hard and crisp – about 6 - 8 minutes.

6 Cool on a wire rack and then store in an airtight tin.

7 Serve with smoked salmon and cream-cheese, smoked mackerel paté and cornichons, scrambled egg or just to snack on.

INDEX

Almond – *flaked*
Seeded Honey Crackers **85**

Anchovies
Pissaladière **94**

Apple
Sweet Flatbreads **89**

Bacon
Flammkuchen **45**
Fougasse **92**
Staffordshire Oatcakes **86**

Baking Powder
American Style Breakfast
Pancakes **71**
Piadina **46**
Potato Farls **82**

Bananas
Sweet Flatbreads **89**

Bánh Xèo 65

Beansprouts
Bánh Xèo **65**

Butter
Sweet Flatbreads **89**

Butter – *clarified (Ghee)*
Naan Bread **51**
Stuffed Parathas **67**

Butter – *melted*
American Style Breakfast
Pancakes **71**
Classic Pancakes **59**
Potato Farls **82**

Carrots
Lahmacun **49**

Cheese
Fougasse **92**
Khachapuri **78**
Socca **55**
Staffordshire Oatcakes **86**

Chocolate – *milk*
Sweet Flatbreads **89**

Chillies
Lahmacun **49**
Stuffed Parathas **67**

Chilli Jam
Socca **55**

Coca 57

Cornflour (*Cornstarch*)
Bánh Xèo **65**

Cream – *double (heavy)*
Sweet Flatbreads **89**

Créme Fraîche
Flammkuchen **45**

Eggs
American Style Breakfast
Pancakes **71**
Classic Pancakes **59**
Khachapuri **78**
Sweet Flatbreads **89**
Yorkshire Puddings **72**

Flammkuchen 45

Flatbreads
– *basic* **42**
– *sweet* **89**

Flour
Ingredients **31**

Flour – *00*
Biga **75**
Flammkuchen **45**
Foccaccia **75**
Mannaeesh **81**
Msemmen **60**
Piadina **46**

Flour – *gram/chickpea*
Socca **55**

Flour – *plain (all purpose)*
American Style Breakfast
Pancakes **71**
Classic Pancakes **59**   Naan Bread **51**   Potato Farls **82**
Staffordshire Oatcakes **86**
Stuffed Parathas **67**
Yorkshire Puddings **72**

Flour – *rice*
Bánh Xèo **65**

Flour – *rye*
Rye Crispbreads **97**

Flour – *strong white*
Basic Flatbread **42**
Coca **57**
Fougasse **92**
Khachapuri **78**
Lahmacun **49**
Naan Bread **51**
Pissaladière **94**
Pitta Bread **53**
Sweet Flatbreads **89**

Flour – *wholemeal*
Lahmacun **49**
Pitta Bread **53**
Seeded Honey Crackers **85**
Staffordshire Oatcakes **86**
Stuffed Parathas **67**

Foccaccia 75

Fougasse 92

Garlic
Bánh Xèo **65**
Lahmacun **49**

Gluten free
Socca **55**
Bánh Xèo **65**

Golden Linseed
Rye Crispbreads **97**

Hazelnuts
Sweet Flatbreads **89**

Herbs & Spices
– *cinnamon*
Sweet Flatbreads **89**
– *coriander*
Bánh Xèo **65**
Lahmacun **49**
Stuffed Parathas **67**
– *cumin*
Socca **55**
Stuffed Parathas **67**
– *fennel seeds*
Rye Crispbreads **97**
Seeded Honey Crackers **85**
– *marjoram*
Foccaccia **75**
Za'atar **81**
– *mixed dried herbs*
Foccaccia **75**
– *mint*
Bánh Xèo **65**
Za'atar **81**
– *nigella seeds*
Pitta Bread **53**
– *parsley*
Lahmacun **49**
– *poppy seeds*
Seeded Honey Crackers **85**
– *sage*
Fougasse **92**
– *sesame seeds*
Seeded Honey Crackers **85**
Za'atar **81**
– *sumac*
Lahmacun **49**
Za'atar **81**
– *sunflower seeds*
Seeded Honey Crackers **85**
– *thyme*
Khachapuri **78**
Pissaladière **94**
Za'atar **81**
– *turmeric*
Bánh Xèo **65**
Stuffed Parathas **67**

Honey
Seeded Honey Crackers **85**

Khachapuri 78

Lamb - *minced*
Lahmacun **49**

Lahmacun **49**

Lard
Piadina **46**

Lettuce
Bánh Xèo **65**

Mannaeesh **81**

Milk
American Style Breakfast
Pancakes **71**
Classic Pancakes **59**
Staffordshire Oatcakes **86**
Sweet Flatbreads **89**
Yorkshire Puddings **72**

Milk – *coconut*
Bánh Xèo **65**

Msemmen **60**

Mushrooms
Bánh Xèo **65**

Naan Bread **51**

Oatmeal
Staffordshire Oatcakes **86**

Oil – *olive*
Foccacia **75**
Fougasse **92**
Khachapuri **78**
Mannaeesh **81**
Pissaladière **94**
Socca **55**
Za'atar **81**

Oil – *sunflower*
Bánh Xèo **65**
Lahmacun **49**
Msemmen **60**
Staffordshire Oatcakes **86**
Stuffed Parathas **67**
Yorkshire Puddings **72**

Olives
Pissaladière **94**

Onions
Flammkuchen **45**
Fougasse **92**
Pissaladiere **94**
Stuffed Parathas **67**

Onions – *red*
Flammkuchen **45**
Foccacia **75**
Lahmacun **49**

Pancakes
– *classic* **59**
– *american style* **71**

Parathas – *stuffed* **67**

Piadina **46**

Pissaladière **94**

Pitta Bread **53**

Potato – *floury*
Potato Farls **82**
Stuffed Parathas **67**

Potato Farls **82**

Prawns
Bánh Xèo **65**

Rye Crispbreads **97**

Salt
Ingredients **31**

Seeded Honey Crackers **85**

Semolina – *extra fine*
Msemmen **60**

Socca **55**

Spring Onions – *scallions*
Bánh Xèo **65**

Staffordshire Oatcakes **86**

Sugar – *caster*
American Style Breakfast
Pancakes **71**
Msemmen **60**
Sweet Flatbreads **89**

Sugar – *icing*
Sweet Flatbreads **89**

Tomato
Foccacia **75**
Lahmacun **49**

Water
Ingredients **31**

Yeast - *fast acting*
Basic Flatbread **42**
Coca **57**
Flammkuchen **45**
Foccacia **75**
Fougasse **92**
Ingredients **31**
Khachapuri **78**
Lahmacun **49**
Mannaeesh **81**
Msemmen **60**
Naan Bread **51**
Pissaladière **94**
Pitta Bread **53**
Rye Crispbreads **97**
Seeded Honey Crackers **85**
Staffordshire Oatcakes **86**
Sweet Flatbreads **89**

Yoghurt
Lahmacun **49**
Mannaeesh **81**
Naan Bread **51**
Pitta Bread **53**

Yorkshire Puddings **72**

Equipment

Axes
A little about ovens **16**
Essential Equipment **27**

Blowpipe
Essential Equipment **27**

Dough Scrapers
Essential Equipment **26**
Let's go make some
dough! **39**

Eco-lighters
A little about ovens **16**
Essential Equipment **26**

Gauntlets
Essential Equipment **26**

Kitchen Papers – *foil,*
baking, parchment etc
Essential Equipment **27**

Mississippi
How hot is the oven? **20**

Pans
Essential Equipment **27**

Peels & Brushes
Essential Equipment **26**

Safety – *buckets, fire*
extinguisher, fire blanket,
first aid kit etc
Essential Equipment **27**

Thermometers
How hot is the oven? **20**
Essential Equipment **26**

Utensils – *bowls, rolling pins,*
whisks etc
Essential Equipment **27**
Let's go make some
dough! **39**

Wood – *split logs*
A little about ovens **16**
Essential Equipment **27**

MANNA from DEVON
COOKING SCHOOL

WOOD FIRED
FLATBREADS
& PANCAKES

by David & Holly Jones

Many thanks to everyone who has helped us put this book together one way or another –

Nick Hook of Nick Hook Photography for his fabulous photos; what a great eye!
Simon E Blogg of Cherub Consultancy Ltd for steering us to our second great looking book and for being so easy to work with
Laura O'Brien for some of her lovely photos taken on one of our courses
Hayley Reynolds and Harriet Fitzgerald of RAW PR and Alan Depledge of Depledge Media for constantly bigging us up
Val Bird in the office for her extreme patience
Kit and Penny Noble for their sharp eyes and constructive criticism
Maddie Jones for her love of banana and chocolate flat breads!
Edward Jones for a seemingly bottomless supply of super dry wood
Jay Emery of Bushman Burners for his fantastic ovens and boundless enthusiasm
Mike Arkell at Gutenberg Press Ltd for all his help
Anna Norman for pointing us in the right direction
Denise Brough at Nkuku for some of our gorgeous props

All our friends and family for having the recipes tested on them and for all their support
over the years we've been running our cooking school, Manna from Devon

You can see more of what we do via any of these channels

Web - **mannafromdevon.com**   Instagram - **MannafDevon**
Facebook - **Manna from Devon**   Pinterest - **Manna from Devon**
Twitter - **@mannafromdevon**   Tumblr - **Manna from Devon**

and you can email us if you've got any questions - **info@mannafromdevon.com**

Coming soon –
Manna from Devon's Wood Fired Fish and Seafood
Manna from Devon's Wood Fired Steaks and Grilling
Manna from Devon's Wood Fired Roasting & Braising
Manna from Devon's Wood Fired Bread
Manna from Devon's Wood Fired Cakes, Biscuits and Pastries

And of course
Manna from Devon's Wood Fired Pizza